W9-AFB-205

FREEDOM
AND DESPAIR

This book is by an author
you admire to an author
and friend I admire.
Love
Soryl

FREEDOM AND AND DESPAIR

Notes from the South Hebron Hills

David Shulman

The University of Chicago Press
Chicago and London

The University of Chicago Press, Chicago 60637
The University of Chicago Press, Ltd., London
© 2018 by The University of Chicago
All rights reserved. No part of this book may be used or repro-
duced in any manner whatsoever without written permission,
except in the case of brief quotations in critical articles and
reviews. For more information, contact the University of Chicago Press, 1427 E. 60th St., Chicago, IL 60637.
Published 2018
Printed in the United States of America

27 26 25 24 23 22 21 20 19 18   1 2 3 4 5

ISBN-13: 978-0-226-56651-1 (cloth)
ISBN-13: 978-0-226-56665-8 (paper)
ISBN-13: 978-0-226-56679-5 (e-book)
DOI: https://doi.org/10.7208/chicago/9780226566795.001.0001

Earlier versions of some portions of this book appeared in
Manoa 20, no. 2 (2008) and in the *Journal of Human Rights
Practice* 6, no. 3 (November 2014).

Library of Congress Cataloging-in-Publication Data

Names: Shulman, David Dean, 1949– author.
Title: Freedom and despair : notes from the South Hebron
   hills / David Shulman.
Description: Chicago ; London : The University of Chicago
   Press, 2018. | Includes bibliographical references and index.
Identifiers: LCCN 2017055604 | ISBN 9780226566511 (cloth :
   alk. paper) | ISBN 9780226566658 (pbk. : alk. paper) | ISBN
   9780226566795 (e-book)
Subjects: LCSH: Arab-Israeli conflict—1993—Peace. |
   Peace movements—Israel. | Pacifists—Israel. | Palestinian
   Arabs—Government policy—Israel. | Palestinian Arabs—
   Government policy—Moral and ethical aspects. | Ta'ayush
   (Organization)—Political activity. | West Bank—Social
   conditions—21st century. | Palestinian Arabs—West Bank—
   Hebron—Social conditions.
Classification: LCC DS119.76 .S7833 2018 | DDC 956.94/2—dc23
LC record available at https://lccn.loc.gov/2017055604

♾ This paper meets the requirements of ANSI/NISO
Z39.48–1992 (Permanence of Paper).

In Memoriam
Isa (Mahmud) Sleby of Beit Ummar, 1953–2012
a man of peace

and for the activists of Ta'ayush

and for my grandchildren, in the
hope they will know truth and peace

CONTENTS

1

ON THE USEFULNESS
OF DESPAIR

> Only a soul full of despair can ever attain serenity and, to be in
> despair, you must have loved a good deal and still love the world.
> —BLAISE CENDRARS

There is action, and there is thinking about action. The two
are sometimes at odds. Acting, doing what one can, the best
one can, is (for me) the easy part. It feels good. You are with
real people. Often it all takes place outdoors in some ravishing
setting rendered less ravishing by human ugliness and cruelty;
there is an adversary to be confronted or even, sometimes, with
luck, overcome. The simple physical business of moving, walking, climbing a hill, racing to help, your blood flowing faster,
your breathing fuller—all this is its own reward. We were not
created to be sitting inside in front of a screen. I like the feel
of the wind on my skin in the South Hebron hills, the dusty
taste of the air, the active business of doing, the intense moral
satisfaction of taking a stand, especially when risk is involved.

That's the easy part. The hard part is the nagging sense of
futility and despair. I want to explore the meaning of those feelings and of the dilemmas they present to us. I know I'm not the
only one to feel, all too often, like I'm battering at windmills.

I've been active in Ta'ayush—Arab-Jewish Partnership—
for the last fifteen years. I've been in South Hebron and elsewhere in Palestine probably hundreds of times. From the start,
we established a special connection with the shepherds and
subsistence farmers of South Hebron. They're a small population, a few thousand, clinging fiercely to the land in the face
of immense pressure by a state that seeks to drive them away
and by the often violent, and insatiably greedy, Israeli settlers
who have been planted in their midst, *on* their lands. We've
stood by the South Hebron Palestinians and even helped a
little, but it's their astonishing, everyday courage and tenac-
ity that explain why they're still there, against all odds. If you
want to read more about the situation in this area and how it
evolved, you can find more information in my book *Dark Hope*.
There is perhaps something to be said for the fact that we've
concentrated our efforts, over years, largely in this one area,
although all of us have experience, often extensive, in other
parts of the occupied territories. I think the Palestinians' situation in South Hebron, while objectively terrible, is still somewhat better than that of Palestinians in the central and northern
West Bank, where there is less of a steady, ongoing presence of
Israeli peace activists.

At the beginning, the futility quotient was very low. In fact,
we were usually euphoric. Everything was new. It may sound
strange, but it's true, nevertheless, that like most Israelis—
including those firmly in the peace camp, on the left—I had
only the most rudimentary experience of Palestinian life and
Palestinian people until 1988–89, when the early dialogue
groups sprung up. The first strong tastes came at that time:
spending a day in Beit Sahour, south of Jerusalem; eating with
our hosts in the village; sometimes sleeping overnight in their
homes; seeing the world as they saw it, confronting the sol-

diers and the police together with them. A world opened up for us. All this deepened immeasurably in the early years of the second Intifada, under the emergency conditions that were in force everywhere in the territories. Now there was action of a far more radical kind—pushing our way past the army blockades, facing the violence of the soldiers and the settlers, finding circuitous and ingenious routes to our friends in the villages, marching together, bringing food and medical supplies, breaking down the roadblocks with our bare hands. It was sometimes dangerous, but the rewards were immediate. And there were many of us: the first time I was in South Hebron, in early 2002, I was one of some 250 activists, and large-scale actions like that were more or less the norm. We thought (I'm a little embarrassed to admit this) that we were the catalysts for what would, perhaps, someday become a mass movement for peace.

We were wrong.

We know the reality all too well. We know what we're up against. The vast machinery of the Occupation has proved remarkably resilient so far, certainly capable of containing our acts of solidarity and struggle, both on the ground and in the courts. We haven't given up, we'll never give up, but I, for one, am haunted by those feelings I mentioned.

Let me give you an example. Take, first, the trivial business of getting out of bed before dawn on a winter morning in order to leave for South Hebron. It's very tempting to stay in bed beside my wife, Eileen. And it's not just a matter of what's comfortable; going to South Hebron means I won't see my grandchildren that day, I won't have time to be with Eileen, of course I won't get to everything I need to do for work, and I won't rest, an art I have so far fruitlessly tried to cultivate. I'm not complaining: it's a choice I happily make, in fact I should be in the territories much more often, what am I doing living my life as if it were really mine when my country and my people are inflicting grievous pain on another people? I know I can never be free in any meaningful way if they are not free. This is the task that has been given me and that I have chosen. If you hear an undertone of guilt, I won't deny it—it's a kind of default, not just for me—but nonetheless I think I can say with confidence that it is not from guilt that I go to South Hebron.

But the real problem with getting out of bed before dawn is the insistent, unnerving inner voice that says: *It's all for nothing. It's anyway a lost cause. We can't make much of a difference. A handful of well-intentioned activists are no match for the malevolent system firmly in place in the territories. A monumental crime is going on, literally hour by hour, and we are not able to stop it. We are banging our heads against a wall. No one even notices what we do. The Israeli public couldn't care less. The international press is generally unaware of or indifferent to our existence. Our victories, such as they are, are minute, our ultimate defeat certain.* And so on. This voice is astonishingly versatile in its range and cleverness. It's much smarter than I am. So why not stay in bed?

But I always go anyway, and I'll tell you why.

First, let me make the context in the field more explicit, because it is there—usually after the "action" is over—that despair sometimes seeps through my defenses. So let us take a real, quite common situation that I have experienced many times. At Umm al-Ara'is, just under the "illegal outpost" of Chavat Yair, there is a fertile wadi—a narrow valley at the base of the hills—whose fields belong (some individually, some collectively) to the extended al-'Awad family. The settlers have stolen them. But since the al-'Awad family has by no means given up on these lands, the Civil Administration has declared the wadi to be "in dispute." This means, translated into practical terms, that settlers continue to have open access to the fields, while their true owners are forbidden to come near them. For over five years now, each week the Palestinian owners march down the hill into the fields, together with Ta'ayush and international activists, to publicly demonstrate their claim. Invariably, soldiers are waiting with an order turning the wadi into a Closed Military Zone; they then proceed to chase the Palestinians—men, women, and children—and the other activists out of it, back up the hill. Sometimes they arrest one or two activists (not so long ago they arrested ten, including a child nursing at its mother's breast). The whole process has acquired a ritualistic aspect. We march into the fields, there is the moment of confrontation—sometimes compounded by the infuriating presence of the settlers—we argue, and in the end we follow the Palestinians in retreat. It feels terrible. We have seen, on occasion, even more savage acts by the soldiers. In November 2013 they joined the settlers and policemen in attacking the activists; many children were beaten. Verbal violence—often incredible in its sheer, obstinate inhumanity—is routine.

Let me say it again: I have been driven off many fields in South Hebron by soldiers who are following their orders, and each time this expulsion is like an open wound in the heart. Incidentally, such acts by the soldiers are expressly illegal according to the ruling of the Israel Supreme Court, but in South Hebron the court is a very distant, nebulous entity. There is only one law there: the law of the gun.

For a while, in the spring–summer of 2015, it looked as if the al-'Awad family might win their struggle and recover some large chunk of land. They were allowed to cultivate and harvest one section of the wadi. The Civil Administration even sent the army, after innumerable delays and excuses, to demolish the fifteen or so greenhouses that the settlers had put up on the stolen land. We thought that we might well be able to halt, at this one tiny point, the remorseless process of expulsion and dispossession that is the norm throughout the territories. We've had many small successes of this sort. So to speak of "futility" is rather out of place. Nonetheless, it *feels* futile. My heart sinks: *Not again.* . . . Despair rises in my stomach, a sick feeling compounded of various elements like rage, disgust, insult, helplessness, and the memories of earlier, familiar traumas. It is not for myself that I feel this despair but for the Palestinians whose pain I have made my own. Sometimes I remind myself at such moments that there is a rational, practical logic that makes it possible, and necessary, for us to undergo this humiliation. It's good to bear it in mind.

In the spring of 2016 the Israeli Supreme Court ruled on this case—or rather, it decided not to rule but to rely on what it called, with touching optimism, the professional judgment of the Civil Administration. This decision not to decide is the equivalent of giving a burglar jurisdiction over a house he has just invaded.

The story of Umm al-Ara'is is not yet over. Sa'id al-'Awad, who has led the campaign there, still hopes that justice will triumph and the land will be restored. It is not impossible that he is right. Still, it is not for pragmatic reasons that I have marched, and will march again, into the wadi at Umm al-Ara'is.

I do it without thinking very much about the results. I do it because—this is what I say to myself in those moments, if I say anything to myself at all—it is the right thing to do, and also the only thing I can do. I do it because it makes me a little freer, makes me feel like a human being. I do it for its own sake. And I want to say something more about the choice to act on moral grounds, as best one can, without romanticizing the choice in any way or turning it into something heroic, which it most definitely is not. In fact, romanticizing it is the one sure way to undermine it and siphon away its value.

Even to think of this work in terms of measurable results (as I did just a few paragraphs ago) is somehow to distort the impulse. Of course, we're human: how can we *not* occasionally calculate the successes we've had, some of them rather salient, like the return home of the exiled villagers of Bi'r al-'Id on the eastern ridge overlooking the desert and their survival there, with our help, in the face of the usual brutal harassment by soldiers and settlers. There are some things we can be proud of. But the functional side of it all is, in a certain sense, secondary to a deeper motivation, which does not depend on tangible results, certainly not in a short-term perspective.

Wittgenstein famously said something along these lines in *Tractatus Logico-Philosophicus* 6.422: "The first thought in setting up an ethical law of the form 'thou shalt . . .' is: And what if I do not do it. But it is clear that ethics has nothing to do with punishment and reward in the ordinary sense. This question as to the consequences of an action must therefore be irrelevant. . . . There must be some sort of ethical reward and ethical punishment, but this must lie in the action itself."

I think when I first read this passage, many years ago, I didn't understand it even on the simplest possible level. There was no way I could have understood it. If I understand it now, it is only because of my own experiences in the South Hebron hills. "The consequences of an action must therefore be irrelevant." The word "therefore" has a little sting, or spin, to it; I like it, not because it suggests a logical deduction (though it does) but because it derives from indubitable experience under conditions of rooted moral ambiguity. When the soldiers threaten me, and I stand up to them, not giving way easily, and even more when they arrest me, I sometimes feel an unexpected happiness, though that may not be the only thing I'm feeling. Like anyone else, I react badly when my physical freedom is revoked. That was one reason I hated the army. But I, like so many others, have discovered empirically the immense difference between external and internal freedom.

At such moments, one's sense of freedom is so overpowering that it is literally impossible to think about the actual results of the action, and the notion of futility is as remote as the moon. I will have more to say about this later on in this book.

But speaking of the ground for action and the ethics of action, I think it's time to reclaim despair, which is as good a ground as any and better than most. Since the results are not the point, despair has a role to play. One despairs: the wickedness is all too present and effective, we cannot stem the tide with our bodies or our words, we confront a faceless system embodied in the faces of the soldiers and bureaucrats and settlers that we meet on the hills. I recommend despair as a place to start. It is in the nature of acting, of doing the right thing, that despair recedes at least for a moment, and its place is taken by something else: hopeless hope, for example. Those who work these furrows know that hope is not contingent. Sometimes the worse things get, the more hope there is, for hope is an act of the deeper self, or the freer part of the person, what some would call a spiritual act, though "spiritual" is not a word I use. In this sense, hope bears no relation to the superficial, mentalistic mode called optimism.

What about the everyday, all-too-familiar kind of despair that saps our strength and may render us unable to act? There is always good reason to feel despair about oneself. Our self-indulgence, our rationalizations, our compromises, our laziness are usually transparent to the inner eye. How could we not despair? And, at such moments, do we have a choice?

Yes. Good despair starts at this point. Good despair drives me from bed on a Saturday morning. There is a movement in the self that goes beyond reflection. The same place in me that knows that I am free and can taste this freedom at rare moments—and this is our most fundamental knowledge of ourselves—is the place that sees where I could go, if only I stopped hesitating and thinking about futility. One very gently and compassionately puts aside the hesitation, even as the futility chorus begins its crescendo. One may need despair, the good despair, to put hesitation aside. Then, for a few moments, one can act, doubt and all.

As the pre-Islamic poet al-Harith ibn Hilliza said, "Nothing consoles you like despair."[1] Not everything that comes into the mind or heart can be used, but I can use my despair; it is, in fact, more to the point, more to the purpose, than many other inner states. It is a friend if I use it wisely. If I use it at a moment when I feel it most keenly—say, for example, when I have just been driven off a certain Palestinian field for the twentieth time, or when I see the soldiers humiliating the owner of the field and I know I can't stop them, or when the soldiers join in with the settlers in beating us and our friends—if I use my despair well in those moments, not expecting immediate, tangible success in the task at hand, indeed not expecting anything, I am likely to feel a little different: not so alone in the world anymore. The despair itself binds me to the victim, my friend; I take him or her into myself; that may be enough. Their suffering is mine, and neither mine nor theirs is in vain. Despair may also par-adoxically bind me at such moments to what remains of the potential decency of the perpetrator, who is betraying his own deeper nature.

Sometimes on those Saturday mornings I say such things to myself as I walk to Gan Hapaamon, where the transit leaves for

South Hebron. It's hopeless, I say, but not in vain. It's not about the result. It's not even about that intoxicating sense of freedom. It's not "about" anything except the intrinsic goodness that sometimes infuses good despair, which transmutes itself into something that cannot be denied. A certain directness and lack of drama are needed for it to work. Despair and delight may thus oddly go hand in hand if the delight does away with our residual self-indulgence, though not, perhaps, with that evergreen voice of doubt.

Perhaps if I didn't despair, I wouldn't keep going down to South Hebron. I'd let others do it for me. The whole point is that the despair is mine, a personal business; thus the act, too, must be mine.

2

A TASTE OF
SOUTH HEBRON

July 23, 2007, Yata, Palestine: Widad's Wedding

For once, some good news. Widad Nawajah is getting married. She's thirty-six years old, far past the usual marriageable age for girls in Palestine. There's not much romance in the match; her bridegroom is twenty-six and in need of a bride, so these two people from the South Hebron hills, where the pool of potential partners is very small, have been paired by their families. One of the uncles tells me the whole story, sparing no detail, as I sit with the men in the long, sparsely furnished sitting room in Yata. Marriage is a certain kind of business; life is hard enough for these people, our friends from the caves and *khirbehs*; let us then celebrate as best we can, glad for a moment of respite from the endless struggle to survive in the face of the settlers and the soldiers and the sun and the rocky soil.

Widad comes from Susya, and we have known her and her family for years. Susya: where thirteen impoverished joint families are clinging tenaciously to the dry hilltop and a few fields that are all that is left to them of their vast ancestral lands. Susya, where tomorrow or the next day the army bulldozers may turn up to wreck the small encampment of Palestinian tents and huts. Last month the Israeli Supreme Court threw out the appeal by the Susya Palestinians against the demolition orders pending against their homes—on technical, bureaucratic grounds. Are we near the end of the Susya story? They have been expelled repeatedly from their homes and fields; this next expulsion could be the last.

Widad is from Susya but her bridegroom is from Yata, now the largest town in the South Hebron hills. Not so long ago Yata was hardly more than a village; today it spills over the golden-brown hilltops for miles—many refugees from the caves and elsewhere have come to rest, for now, in the town. Yata is poor, dry, unfinished, littered with the inevitable flotsam and jetsam of modern Palestine—the wrecks of old cars, the dusty grocery shops, the graffiti left over from the last election, the sheep and goats and barefoot children, the disintegrating old stone houses dwarfed by ugly, recent buildings, the medieval ruins overgrown by scraggly grass and thorns. We drive through the suq with its open vegetable stalls, its vendors of trinkets and T-shirts; we hear the afternoon call to prayer. The sun has burned the streets white, exposing potholes, scattered refuse, the peeling plaster of the facades.

Nasser leads us through twisting lanes to the houses of the groom's family, a series of three or four tall, adjacent buildings, with parking space below for the sheep. Anat, Liat, and Becca, all veteran activists who know the families well, are led upstairs to the women's chambers, where Widad is sitting or standing in state; I am piloted to the male zone next door. I greet each of the many relatives in turn, uttering blessings. I take my seat on a low divan, with Hafez, our friend from Twaneh, to my right, Nasser to my left. Young boys serve Turkish coffee in small glasses carried on brass platters. On the wall there are the usual calligraphic verses from the Qur'an. One of the elders, a striking, dignified man in white robe and keffiyeh, fingers his prayer beads. We wait, mostly in silence.

It is a neutral, undemanding silence, and after a while I feel myself relaxing into it. I realize that my task today is simply to be here, to be present, to wait with patience for whatever happens. At first the standard anxiety of the harried Israeli bubbles up as a question, which I manage to frame in Arabic, to Nasser: "What is going to happen today?" He finds the question comic. "What will happen? *'Urs*—a wedding!" He shrugs. I think it over and realize that this most probably means some ritual meal. I must fulfill my duty as a guest. Meanwhile I sip the coffee, listen keenly to scraps of Arabic conversation, try to read the Qur'anic verses on the wall. Eventually my mind lets go of words and other surface things.

It is like what the Afghanis told the Americans in the distant days when the Taliban were fighting the Soviets and the Americans had come to help them: "You have all the clocks, but we have all the time." Time laps at my eyes, settles into pools at my feet. Maybe there is enough of it to cushion and absorb all the suffering. I wonder. From time to time a new male enters into this space, speaks the greetings, sits down; occasionally the newcomer speaks. Thus a young, vigorous man rehearses last night's story from Susya, that is, home. I have already heard it in bits and pieces on the way down here, but now there is a fuller narrative, told with a strange detachment and economy.

It began around 11:00 p.m. Our friend Ezra, the real hero of South Hebron, was passing Susya on his way back to Jerusalem when he saw a light in one of the Palestinian fields. He knew at once what it meant. Israeli settlers were doing what they do so naturally, as if it were God's overt command: they were stealing another field. They had already managed to lay down several rows of plastic irrigation pipes, a clear statement of ownership in this area; when the Palestinians would wake in the morning, they would discover that the settlers' boundary had been extended by another sizable chunk, at their expense. Another irreparable loss. Ezra called the police in Kiryat Arba. But the settlers are tuned in to the police network—in effect, the two groups work hand in hand—so as soon as they heard the call, dozens of young settler toughs descended on Ezra, screaming curses, threatening to kill him. Then the soldiers arrived, and also a few of the Palestinians, seeking to protect their field. The settlers attacked Ezra's car with rocks and other weapons, but miraculously he wasn't hurt; he was, so he tells me later, beginning to become really afraid, a rare experience for this truly intrepid man.

"What time did it happen?" the elder asks. "Around 11." "And there were lots of police and soldiers?" "Yes, lots." What more is there to ask? All of it is utterly routine. The people of Susya live in terror. Even terror becomes routine. I study their faces. These are men, with the sensitive pride of the Mediterranean male. Their story is one of continuous humiliation, of agonies of impotence; they cannot protect their own fields, their homes have been taken away from them over and over, they are easy prey for the settlers with their guns; they ache the man's ache, the one that has no healing. I hear it in the broken, staccato language that embodies memory after memory, last night's now added to this unending series of insults. Thanks to Ezra, last night's events ended relatively well. The field is still theirs. What will happen tonight?

Lunch arrives: platters of yellow rice decked with joints of lamb, dripping with fat. Three or four men eat from each platter. The chunks of bone and meat look only barely removed from the living sheep, whom perhaps we saw on our way in. You have to tear the meat off with your fingers, but there are big spoons for the rice: a greasy business. Tea is served shortly thereafter. Now suddenly one of the newcomers is curious about me. Where am I from? Al-Quds. What do I do? I teach languages. Suddenly they remember: You're the one from India, the doctor from the university. Yes. I admit it. But I'm not from India, I say, I'm Israeli. I'm from Ta'ayush, the peace organization. They nod. Nasser's young son, Adam, suddenly wants to know: Did I serve in the army? He's caught me. I'd like to deny it—here, in the presence of people for whom the army means occupation, slavery, the constant nightmare. I feel ashamed.

Ehud arrives together with another Ta'ayush contingent. We sit and talk. He was at the Supreme Court session last week that decided against the Susya people. He describes it graphically but no less laconically than the report we just heard of last night's events. The state attorney claimed, of course, that the Palestinians of Susya were a security threat to the settlers—hence they should be removed. "Where will they go?" the judges asked. The state replied: "We don't know. They are unfortunates, *miskenim*." The state also doesn't much care, and the judges, their duty done, their conscience clean enough, threw out the case. Soldiers follow orders; judges follow rules.

It is, as anyone can see, a fairly ordinary day in South Hebron. All this is the stuff of daily experience. But there are happy moments, too. A wedding, not perhaps the perfect sort one dreams of, but still it is a day of celebration. Tired of the all-male company, which has lapsed back into silence, tired of this plethora of time going nowhere, neither backward or forward, I climb up to pay my respects to the bride. Widad stands by the window in a white dress that seems composed of endless layers of flared, starched cotton. She has one glass eye. She looks a bit nonplussed, but she smiles warmly when she sees me, she shakes my hand, almost winks. Much attention has been lavished on her black hair. Dozens of women, mostly in black, with deeply grooved, wrinkled faces, glistening eyes, sit on stools along the walls. Apparently, I missed the dancing. Tonight they will take the bride in procession to the nuptial quarters, three houses away. She will surely cry. From the roof-top where I stand, I study the purple hills in the distance, the green pines that hide the violent settlement of Chavat Maon, just across the road, the vastness of the afternoon sky. Susya is almost visible to the south, a tiny dot amid the stones and thorns. It is not, I think, about happiness; happiness is more than we can expect. It is about waiting—one more day, then another, there is never an end to the days—without hope.

December 1, 2007, Tuba

Tuba: another minute, almost invisible point on the map; an-other village of black tents and wobbly huts and a well and a few caves carved into the barren hillside, almost hovering in space on the edge of the desert that cascades and flows, white yellow and brown, all the way down to the Dead Sea. In the distance you can see the purple mountains of Moab in Jordan. There is not, I think to myself, a more stunning vista in the world. A camel regards us skeptically. What are all these people doing here? Dogs bark. Goats bleat. The wind whips your eyes, your hair. Some hundred souls live in Tuba—a simple, impov-erished existence, but poverty is not the problem. They live in terror, and they are terribly alone.

I was far from confident that we'd make it as far as the vil-lage. For the last two weeks, we were haunted by the thought that the army would block us somewhere along Route 60, the main north-south route from Jerusalem, and the long days of preparation and planning would all be wasted. Many people were by now involved, including famous poets and novelists and scholars who had agreed to join us; in the end the sheer number of volunteers surprised us. This time, for some reason, we touched a cord. The four buses—from Jerusalem, Tel Aviv, and Beer-Sheva—are packed with people. Many of them, to my delight, are new to me, young faces never seen before in the South Hebron hills.

It's not every day that several hundred activists, Israelis and Palestinians, march together up the rocky path from Twaneh toward Tuba. In fact, this is the first time. It has the odd sense of blessing, defiant, angry, oxymoronic. Of course, the soldiers and the police are waiting for us halfway up the hill. They block our path, they inform us that this is—as always—a closed military area, that we are breaking the law, that we must turn around and go home at once or face arrest. There are lots of them, with their jeeps and command cars and armored half-tracks, including the particularly ominous one that is designed as a mobile prison, with little slits in the armor plating so the detainees can breathe. Armored vehicles are never charming, but this one—which I know from inside—is ugly beyond belief, a kind of archaic metal monster left over from some desperate, distant struggle. I guess they're expecting to arrest quite a few of us.

We enter into negotiations: we have come to visit our friends in Tuba, to protect them as they plow their fields, we are, after all, in Area C, which Israelis can visit legally, so why are they trying to stop us? The sun has broken through the winter clouds, it's getting hot, the police and soldiers are adamant, menacing, but suddenly we remember to ask them to show us the signed military order closing off this zone, as the law requires. To our amazement, they have forgotten to bring it along. It will take them a few minutes to prepare it on the spot, and this is our opportunity; without that small piece of paper, they are helpless, weapons and all, so we at once break through the barrier and rush uphill—and soon there is a long, jagged line of our people, together with the Twaneh and Tuba contingent, weaving a path among the thorns and rocks toward the dusty fields. Yehuda, Roee, Raanan, and Ehud, all veterans of these hills, are leading the way; Moshe, from the Combatants for Peace, is keeping an eye out for stragglers and trying to mold the mass of people into some almost coherent form. The soldiers snarl and threaten and try to hold us back, but they have lost this round. There is no way they will be able to stop all of us, even if the order arrives.

And here it is again, that heady feeling, like no other, of being free, carefree, utterly indifferent to their yells and snarls, happy in this moment, happy to be with these people who are doing something that is good and right, who have gone through and beyond the fear and the ingrained habit of obedience and who are probably enjoying this now as much as I am—a little drunk, perhaps, on so much freedom. The soldiers are pushing us to the right and downhill as we round the bend at the periphery of Chavat Maon, home to the most vicious of the Israeli settlers in this region, the crazed enemies of our Palestinian friends. The settlers are waiting for us, as expected, in their white Shabbat clothes and their inflated skullcaps, but they are clearly cowed by our numbers, unable, for once, to attack. They content themselves with screaming curses: "I pray that the Hamas will kill you first among the Jews!" "It's because of you that there is terrorism," etc., etc. We've heard them all before.

By now I am walking with Menachem Brinker, philosopher, literary historian, one of the founders of the Israeli peace movement; he is over seventy and the march is not easy for him. He has slowed to the point that he and I are almost alone, face to face with the settlers—the main body of our people has moved rapidly over the hills toward the Tuba fields—so we have plenty of time to savor the curses that are coming our way. Menachem finds them not uninteresting. The Jews, he said, had first to learn—decades ago—to overcome their deep passivity, to rediscover how to act in the world, defend themselves, fight back; and this lesson they truly learned. Now they have to overcome the fascism that comes with blind, autistic power: witness the settlers, their primitive malice, their adoration of brute compulsion. I speak of the Combatants for Peace, our partners in today's action; they are a young, energetic group composed of ex-soldiers, on the Israeli side, and former fighters in the Palestinian organizations (Fatah, the Popular Front, and others). They have renounced violence and are committed to working together for peace. I have seen them, I say to Menachem, here in South Hebron—seen how they have moved from the early, joyful stage of dialogue with one another to the point of actively confronting the settlers and facing off, together, against the police and the soldiers. It's an inevitable progression, once you have tasted the realities on the ground. Yes, says Menachem, with a bitter smile; you begin down here with action motivated by the love of mankind and end up by hating the settlers.

By the time we rejoin our companions, the Palestinians have managed to plow two fields, one with a rusty tractor, the second with the time-honored donkey and metal plow. Police and soldiers are everywhere, and soon a heavyset settler appears, on cue, to give them their orders that, as always, are obeyed: the plowing must stop. The police rush to confiscate the keys to the Palestinian tractor, and suddenly they want to know who *really* owns this field that the settlers, naturally, claim; not another clod must be turned over until maps are brought from headquarters, hours away, and the rival claims adjudicated. As if there were any grounds for doubt: every field on these dessicate hills belongs to the Palestinian villagers, and every such field is potential plunder for the settlers. We argue with the police, there is shouting and fussing and confusion; the activists wander up and down the slope in the afternoon sun, wondering what to do next.

Word filters in that, in revenge for our successful démarche, settlers have descended upon Twaneh and are assaulting the villagers there. Roee and others rush back to try to help. Another large contingent of Palestinian Combatants for Peace has also arrived in the village, some of them from quite far away, Ramallah, Tulkaram, and this time the police have successfully contained them there; we will have to manage without them. We have known all along that all of this is part of the package, and we asked our hosts, again and again, if they are sure they want us to come here today—since they are certain to be violently attacked by the settlers as soon as we leave, or even before. They were unequivocal: they need us to come, they have nothing more to lose. And the newly plowed fields—what will happen to them tomorrow? The settlers will certainly rampage through them. So why are our friends plowing them? We have to plow, the land is pleading with us, we cannot leave her to die. We must open her to the benefice of rain. Such are the farmer's instincts. As for us, we know that today is but another skirmish in an endless, dreary, daily war. We are not about to give up. In the end, it is a war that we will win.

We gather up our forces for a few words, spoken defiantly into the wind. Yaron Ezrahi, ever the eloquent teacher, has the megaphone and is addressing our Palestinian hosts. "I am an expert in the comparative study of democracies," he says, "and I have come to the conclusion that Israel's form of government is less and less a member of this category. What we see here, in Tuba, is inhuman cruelty perpetrated on innocents. We have come to fight it, and to give you hope." Raanan tells the long story of Tuba's sorrows, the grief that stalks the night, the fright of each new day. When the story is over, we wander farther over the hilltop to Tuba, clinging to the last, steep ridge in the late afternoon light that is already turning crystal, freezing into gold. Lonely, vulnerable Tuba—perhaps today, for a few moments, a little less alone.

Time to go, retracing our steps. We have done what we came to do. I can see it is a good combination, this alliance of Ta'ayush and the Combatants for Peace; perhaps today is but the first of many shared actions in the field. At times the great human mass, slowly moving back toward Twaneh, laps up against the policemen, and there are brief, angry confrontations. We descend into the wadi, climb back up to the footpath circling Chavat Maon. Young settler girls are now standing there, watching us with hate, hurling imprecations. I can't say I care. It has been a day of great happiness—whatever happens tomorrow. But just as we reach the buses and are about to climb in, at this very last moment, news arrives. Settlers have attacked the fifteen-year-old son of our friend 'Umar Jundiyeh, have beaten him badly; and they have also stolen the donkey he was riding.

We call the police, who suggest, with cool disdain, that the young boy in question come to the station in Kiryat Arba, long miles away, in order to fill out forms and submit a complaint. This won't do. By now all of us are tired and eager to head home, but we can't leave the matter of the donkey unresolved.

If you live in a tent or a cave in Tuba, on the edge of the desert, with no access roads to the outer world and the settlers at your throat day after day, a donkey is no small matter. We will have to force some sort of action. So we send the main body of buses off to Jerusalem and Tel Aviv, leaving some forty or fifty of us outside the well-established settlement of Maon. It is here, it seems, that the thieves have hidden the donkey. We prepare to march on Maon.

It's getting dark. A pastel sun appears to shrink deep into itself, diminishing as it dips below the horizon. It's also quite cold by now. The police are anything but happy at this twist in our tactics. They had thought they were rid of us at last, and here we are at the entrance to the settlement, about to burst through the gate. Tires screeching, they pull up in front of us, jump from the cars, lock arms, and slowly, forcefully push us away from the gate. They scream at us, they threaten to arrest us (do they know any other sentences than these?). "And what about the donkey?" we cry back at them. It is a moment of black parody, and no one fails to see the silliness of it all. But can human evil be silly? By now we are chanting in rhythmic Hebrew: "*Ha-hamor hayyav lahzor,*" "The donkey must come home!" Which donkey? It's not clear that we don't mean the police officer in charge who, by now exhausted and exasperated, is shoving us back toward the road. He wants to clear us away, that much is clear, but we're not about to give up until something is done about the donkey. Noblesse oblige.

Wearily, they summon another police van from the Kiryat Arba station. Ezra has meanwhile located the boy who was beaten and brought him to our encampment at the side of Route 60. Reluctantly, the policemen take down his testimony; they even ask him to identify the settlers who attacked him by showing him photos they happen to have with them in the van.

Not that they would act even on a positive identification. Writing down his testimony takes a long time. We scavenge for dry firewood, and soon a fire is blazing. We settle in, drinking in sweet wood-smoke, huddled around the flames. Someone has brought his flute along, and soon the air is light with Bach and Mozart and Hebrew and Arabic folksongs. I know it doesn't sound likely, this utterly surreal setting in the desert with the bonfire, the shrill notes, the policemen pacing back and forth, the darkness sinking into the stones, the evening chill, the sparks and smoke, the beat-up boy, the missing donkey, the unpunished and unpunishable settler thieves—but this is actually the best hour of the day for me, when the final foolishness of it all has broken through to the surface and there is no longer much need, or space, to think.

We laugh, we tell stories. It turns out that this same 'Umar Jundiyeh has previously lost two donkeys to the settlers; the first time it happened, he went to Kiryat Arba to file a complaint, and the police officers told him they couldn't act on the case unless he presented them with a photograph of the donkey. Hillel remembers the Arab tale of the great Caliph Harun al-Rashid, who was speaking with his wife one evening in their bedroom as a poor man, who had lost his donkey and was searching for it everywhere, was resting in a tree outside the open bedroom window. "Take off all your clothes and walk around the room," said the caliph to his wife. "It's wrong," she said. "It's not wrong," said the caliph. So she did as he commanded, as the caliph watched her. "What did you see?" she asked him afterward. "I saw the world and all that is in it," he said. "Ah," cried the poor man outside, listening to their words, "then perhaps you have also seen my donkey."

Why don't we set up an "illegal outpost" of our own, someone asks, here around the bonfire, a peace outpost; we can call it, in the settler's mode, Hamor-El, "Donkey of God." "Those settlers of Chavat Maon," says my son Edan, "why couldn't they just be eccentric hippies who have chosen to live out here in the forest on the hill? Isn't that who they're meant to be? Why do they have to do such terrible things?" He puts the question sweetly, tongue in cheek; but he has touched on the deepest human mystery. "What's taking so long," asks someone else, "why are they keeping that kid in the police van—or are they going to charge him with the crime of losing a donkey and sentence him to jail?" Much stranger things happen in that upside-down world. If you're a Palestinian attacked by settlers, it is *always* your fault. As for the donkey, there's probably not much hope. The good news is that we are together again, together with the villagers, the press, the international volunteers, together also with the new Combatants, and we have been through one more adventure. Always there will be one more and another one after that and so it will go, with the occasional loss of a donkey or, possibly, some more dangerous loss or hurt until one day the furious nightmare of South Hebron comes to an end and the settlers leave and the soldiers also leave and our friends from the caves can go back to their rough and ready lives, without needing us to protect them anymore, and the adventures will cease. I don't think it will happen soon.

April 12, 2008, Umm al-Khair: Eid Suleman al-Hathalin

This is Eid's story, I'm just reporting it. But I need to give you at least a little background. We're in Umm al-Khair, a ramshackle collection of tents and huts and simple stone houses and sheep pens and corrugated shacks that borders, tragically, on the settlement of Carmel in the South Hebron hills. Or rather, historically, Carmel borders on Umm al-Khair, since the lands appropriated for the settlement in the early 1980s all belonged to the Bedouin goat herders and farmers who live on this rocky hill. They bought the land for good money from the original owners in the town of Yata when they fled from Tel Arad in the Negev in the wake of the 1948 war. These days, like everywhere in South Hebron, the Palestinian shepherds of Umm al-Khair face constant depredations from the settlers, who frequently chase them off their historic grazing grounds, hoping to starve them into leaving for good. That's why we're here today—to protect the shepherds, to accompany them as they graze their sheep. It's been the standard South Hebron sort of morning: a large body of police and soldiers turned up to shoo us away, with the usual specious excuses and threats, but we stood our ground, and now the sheep have had their fill, more or less, of the thorny leaves they seem to relish. Eid, a handsome man in his twenties, in a bright yellow T-shirt, leads me into the shade of a tent and starts to speak.

"I was born in Umm al-Khair. Today everyone goes to the hospital to give birth, but my head touched the ground over there, in that stone house. I grew up here. I went to school in the schoolhouse on the opposite ridge. I learned English at school. In tenth grade I stopped, there was no money, but by then I was a 'gentleman' in English. I learned Hebrew from watching television and from books.

This is a Bedouin village. We came from Tel Arad after the first war. My grandfather bought the land. Before he died, he spoke to all of us. He said, 'Sons, grandsons, listen to me. The peaceful way is the only way.' My father followed his advice. He was against violence. He taught us. He spent his life following the goats. But he studied a lot, and he understood. He also learned Hebrew. He told us, 'My sons, if settlers attack us, we don't do what they do. We follow the path of peace.' He died five years ago. He was a man like you.

At first when the settlers came, they would come to drink tea with us, and my grandfather said, 'We are cousins. We want to live without problems.' I saw them building the settlement when I was eight years old. Workers from Gaza did the building. Those were different days. Then the new settlers came, and all the problems.

Today the settler is the king. He drags the whole country and the army after him, just as you would drag a dog. If the settler says to the soldiers, 'Arrest that man,' they'll arrest him. If a settler attacks you and you go to the police to submit a complaint, the police will find all kinds of reasons to block it. They'll waste your time, they'll make you wait and wait, then they'll say, 'We don't have a photograph of the man, there's no identification.'

They attack us all the time. The settler kids throw rocks in the evening. If you're in your home and a rock falls on the metal roof—you see that kind of roof we have?—you hear it, it disturbs you, you don't sleep all night. We're sick of the police. They never arrest a single settler. They don't do anything.

I'm married. I have a three-month-old baby. There's no work. I owe a lot of money for the wedding. I can't work in Tel Aviv, because I'm too young; they won't give permits to anyone under thirty. There's no money, no electricity, no water. We bring water every day from the well on the other hill, half a kilometer away. We have to bring it on a donkey. You know how hard it is in the winter for the donkey? The donkey is not like a vehicle. We can get water from a pipe farther away, near Maon, but we have a debt of ten thousand shekels to the water company; if we don't pay this summer, those dogs in the Palestinian Authority will tell the Civil Administration to cut off the water, like they did last summer.

This year there was no rain. Soon the few green leaves in the wadi will be gone. We will have to buy food for the animals from the dealers in Yata. It costs a huge amount of money. My father brought food from Yata for years and ran up a debt of thirty thousand shekels. They demand the money. How can we pay thirty thousand shekels? I am carrying this debt on my shoulders, but there's no way we can pay. My father had 120 goats, but only thirty are left.

We're five families here in Umm al-Khair, about seventy people. Someone sent us a solar heating unit from Germany. That was ten years ago. It doesn't work anymore. There's no way we can get electricity here. But this is where I want to live. My land is here.

I know on my own body that there is no solution except to wage war for peace. Not a war with bullets and rifles and bombs. That isn't right. There has to be a party of Palestinians and Israelis for peace. The settlers and the Palestinian extremists—we have to change their heads, the way they think. If a settler gets killed, who pays the price? Me and you. Killing is not the way. This conflict won't be solved by war.

My brother was arrested. He was just walking on the hill, and they arrested him and kept him in jail for three months. My father was arrested, too. That's how it is. If one of us is walking on the path, on his own land, the settlers run after him and attack him. They wanted to do that today, but because you were here, their hands were tied. But maybe when you leave and the police go away, the settlers will hide in the trees and then they'll come. We know they will come.

It's not the soldiers who are bad. There are all kinds. Some are extremist, others vote for Meretz or Labor. They come to drink tea with us, no problem. Sometimes there are good surprises. Once one of us was hurt, deep in the desert. The army sent a helicopter to rescue him! They saved him, and they didn't ask for money. A year ago one of our people had an accident, his car overturned on one of the hills and he was trapped. An army patrol just happened by. God sent that patrol. They called Magen David Adom, they saved him. Once there was an accident on the main road, and some Israelis passing by stopped to help. They took the wounded man, one of us, all the way to Soroka Hospital [in Beer-Sheva]. He was in hospital for thirty days, and we didn't have to pay the hospital any money. When I think of the State of Israel, that is what I see. I don't see the State of Israel in the settler. I put him aside. I see it in the soldiers who sent the helicopter, and I see it in people like you and your friends."

Eid has more to say, but we suddenly get word of an emergency at Umm Zeituna—settlers have again attacked the shepherds. We have to rush there to help. I promise Eid that I'll be back soon. As I'm leaving, an old man, Salim 'Id al-Hathalin, grabs hold of me. He is waving papers—one a receipt from the tax authorities, confirming that he has paid taxes on the lands he owns here in the village; the other a demolition order issued by the Civil Administration against his makeshift tent-cum-hut, which he points out to me as he cries: "Why do they want to destroy my house? Where can I go? Can I go to America? I have nothing, and they want to take that nothing from me. Can you help me? Where am I supposed to go?"

August 16, 2009, Jerusalem District Court: Ezra Nawi

Ezra Nawi's trial is drawing to a close. He's accused of assaulting two Border Policemen during house demolitions at Umm al-Khair, and the judge, Elata Ziskind, has already found him guilty. What's left is sentencing, preceded by character witnesses and closing arguments. I'm here to bear witness on his behalf, along with several other activists and friends. Ezra is Israeli of Iraqi origin, fluent in Arabic; he came to political action slowly, and not from reading books. Then he reinvented nonviolent resistance from his own experience—by trial and error—in the hills of South Hebron.

Here's the context, in brief. In February 2007, the army sent its bulldozers to demolish several of the tin-and-canvas shanties in Umm al-Khair. Ezra was there—he always appears, miraculously on time, wherever he is needed in South Hebron—and, in the best tradition of civil disobedience, he did his best to slow down the demolitions. He threw himself on the ground in front of the bulldozers, and the soldiers had to drag him away. Then he ran into one of the shacks about to be destroyed, and two Border Policemen ran in after him. All this is documented on video that is readily available on the internet. What the camera could not record is what happened in the twenty seconds or so inside the shack. Some days after the event, the Border Policemen claimed that Ezra resisted and also raised his hand against them; he fiercely denies this, and I believe him. I know the man, know his profound aversion to violence of any kind. At the time, they dragged him out and handcuffed him and arrested him. In the video you can see the soldiers mocking him for helping Palestinians; it's not a pretty sight. You can also hear Ezra saying to them: "I was once a sol-dier myself, but I never destroyed a person's home. Here only hatred will be left behind" (https://www.youtube.com/watch?v=ysIaQUJWBdk).

You have to know that if a Palestinian in Umm al-Khair needs to build a home or add a room to his tent or shack, there's vir-tually no chance he'll get a building permit. In all of Area C in the occupied territories (under direct Israeli control), with a

Palestinian population of several hundred thousand souls, on
average only one or two permits are issued each month. Inevitably, people end up building without permits—they usually
have very large families—and just as inevitably, the Civil
Administration issues its demolition orders and then sends
the bulldozers to carry them out. On average, in "good" times,
sixty such orders are issued every month, of which twenty are
carried out. In bad times, there are many more demolitions.
It's happened many times at Umm al-Khair, only a few meters
away from the modern red-roofed villas erected by Israeli
settlers at the Carmel settlement. It happened again on February 14, 2007, when Ezra did whatever he could. I'm sorry I
wasn't there to help him that day.

Anyway, the judge had only the conflicting testimony of
Ezra and the policemen, and naturally she believed the policemen. I was at the trial. I can tell you what my fantasy was that
day in court. Only a fantasy—but still. Here was an opportunity for the judge to say: "Look what the state was doing, and
look at Ezra's attempt to protest. House demolitions in Umm
al-Khair, however legal they may be in some technical sense,
are in fact brute demonstrations of power inflicted on innocents. They also happen to be illegal under international law.
Reality matters and should, at least occasionally, make sense of
the law. When Ezra threw himself down in front of the bulldozers, he may indeed have been hampering a public servant in the
discharge of his duties; but since in this case those duties were
reprehensible, and since there was nothing violent in Ezra's
act, we would do well to see it in its courageous aspect as a
moral statement in the face of oppression." Or something like
that. I didn't expect to hear such words from her, but I mourn
the fact that she didn't say them.

So here we are at 8:00 a.m. in the District Court, Room 324

in the old Russian Compound (built by the Russian Orthodox Palestine Society for Russian pilgrims and clergy between 1859 and 1864). The courtroom is very small, far too small to accommodate all of Ezra's friends and supporters. With the other witnesses, I am exiled to the grimy corridor outside. I've been told by Ezra's experienced lawyer, Lea Tsemel, that I'll have about five minutes, in the course of which I am supposed to explain the history of Gandhian civil disobedience and Ezra's place in this venerable tradition. I've rehearsed in my mind what I want to say and can only hope that they'll give me a chance and that I will find the words. My friend Suchitra has advised me to adopt one of Gandhi's own methods before facing the judge: to pray. In the constant commotion in the corridor—burly policemen passing by loaded down with stacks of shiny handcuffs, clerks pushing trays heavy with files, and quite a few lost souls in search of someone or something undefined—I give it a try.

After an hour or so, I am ushered in. To my left stands the prosecutor, a young Palestinian woman, believe it or not. I smile at Ezra to my right and vaguely take in the faces of a few of my activist colleagues on the benches near the door. Far above me, behind a high wooden bar, sit Justice Ziskind and, at her side, an earnest typist hovering over a computer keyboard. I am advised that I must speak the truth and that I must speak it slowly, as slowly as possible, so the typist can keep up and the transcript will be complete.

"How long have you known the defendant?"

A long time, I say, several decades. He was our plumber. Highly professional. He worked for us for many years, dealt with various emergencies, before I had any inkling of his political views or his activism. But in the last nine years, I am with him regularly in the South Hebron hills, on peace work.

"What can you tell us about him?"

First, I say, I want to emphasize that I have been through many difficult moments with him—attacks by settlers, in particular—and I have never seen him respond to violence with violence. Once in Susya, in 2005, settlers broke a wooden pole over his head, and he stood his ground without hitting back. I was right beside him, and I saw it. I have seen such instances many times. He is committed to nonviolent protest as a way of life and as an ethical discipline.

"Nonviolent protest?"

"I mean the tradition of Mahatma Gandhi and Martin Luther King and Henry David Thoreau."

The typist raises her hands. The judge repeats the first two names. I can see I have to help out, so I spell them: G-a-n-d-h-i. From India, the struggle against British colonialism. M-a-r-t-i-n . . .

Actually, there's an advantage to this pace. It gives you plenty of time to think and also allows you to say everything twice or thrice, which is all to the good. I keep looking at the judge, trying to reach her eyes and, if at all possible, her heart. She remains aloof, impassive. She looks right through me. She looks, in fact, rather bored. She is, however, deeply concerned with helping the typist. She nods to me to go on.

Everyone recognizes, I tell the court, the method, or the way of life, of nonviolent civil disobedience. Ezra Nawi is in this tradition. I see him as belonging to the same honored series as those brave Americans who entered segregated buses together with blacks in the South, fifty years ago, though it was illegal for a black person to be on those buses; or with those who accompanied black children to schools though it was against the law for them to be in all-white schools. We are talking about situations in which nonviolent protest is directed against a system and its rules or actions which may be technically legal but which are in conflict with basic human values and with our conscience as human beings. A man like Ezra Nawi feels he has not only the right but, in fact, a duty to try to oppose such rules.

Most of this has to be repeated several times. The judge is getting restless. I will have to squeeze all the rest into a few sentences at most. But by now I have relaxed enough to think more or less clearly, and I know where I am going.

Mahatma Gandhi, I say, told a British judge in Ahmedabad in 1922: "Noncooperation with evil is as much a duty as cooperation with good." This is the situation we face in the South Hebron hills. I am certain that a day will come when Ezra Nawi's name will be taught in Israeli schools, in the textbooks, as an example of a person who embodied true human values in the dark times that we are living through today.

She's doing her best, the typist, but it's not working. "What kind of times did you say?"

"Dark."

What I really want to say is: No one remembers the name of the British judge who sent Gandhi to jail in 1922 (his name was C. N. Broomfield) or of the judge who imprisoned Henry David Thoreau. But I don't say it. I bite my tongue. Still, I allow myself a parting shot.

There's just one more thing, I say. I'm sixty years old, I have four grandchildren, and I sometimes think that if there is anything that I can be proud of in my life, then it's not the books I have written or the prizes I have won but those moments in South Hebron when I had the privilege of standing beside Ezra Nawi when the settlers attacked.

It feels good to have said it. In fact, I even got to say it twice.

Now the prosecutor cross-examines in musical, Arabic-tinged Hebrew. She wants to know if I know anything about

Ezra's previous convictions. I say they're not relevant. And, she says, you're not impartial, I bet you're angry at the settlers. Sometimes I am, I say, and turn the question back on her: "If someone attacked you, would you not be a little angry, too?" She seems nonplussed at this; I can't help wondering how she feels, arguing against Ezra, crossing the lines. Perhaps she's overcompensating. All the witnesses later report that she kept striving earnestly to impugn Ezra's character. Just doing her job. Or is she? You can't tell me she really believes those Border Policemen and their predictable story. I wonder where she grew up and where she studied law. I guess it's all part of the surreal world of the Israeli courtroom. No one is innocent there, least of all the intricate system that sustains the Occupation and its cruel rules.

I think about what Gandhi wrote in his statement to the judge in Ahmedabad: "The greatest misfortune is that Englishmen and their Indian associates in the administration do not know that they are engaged in crime." Sounds familiar. Most Israelis don't know, or don't want to know; judges included. Some would, no doubt, be incredulous were they to see the reality in the territories as it is. It is, in fact, hard to believe. Then I start to wonder if Gandhian "acts of truth," satyagraha—nonviolent assertion of a moral stance in the face of an immoral system—are really the right method in this Levantine morass. Could it ever soften the heart of even one Israeli soldier? Yes, it can: I know an instance from Bil'in; one of the soldiers stationed in the village, seeing the army's brutal suppression of the villagers' protest at the theft of their lands by the state, has come over to our side and now comes with us to South Hebron. Bil'in was one of the first villages to experiment with Gandhian methods in Palestine (along with nearby Budrus, Abu Dis in east Jerusalem, and others); nonviolent resistance has now spread widely throughout the territories. But will any of this turn the tide? Almost certainly not. Israel does not have the internal resources to make political change. We have the dream of mass civil disobedience in Palestine, led by some charismatic figure still undiscovered. It is still a dream. In the past, the army has shown great talent in turning nonviolent demonstrations into violent ones, which the generals and the politicians much prefer. And yet—there is truly no other way. Violence compounds the evil. And besides: the beauty of Gandhian-style protest is that it needs no further justification; it is right in itself, worth doing for itself, for the sake of truth.

Judge Ziskind dismisses me and I go back to the corridor where Galit, who testified just before me, is sitting with the Hebrew Bible on her lap; she quoted a few relevant verses to the judge. Another young Palestinian lawyer is waiting there, for some reason, and we start to chat. He got his law degree from Al-Quds University in Abu Dis. The Israel Bar Association recognizes degrees from Al-Quds, but the Israel Council for Higher Education won't give Al-Quds graduates the same academic rank as others because Al-Quds is situated partly within and partly outside Jerusalem's municipal border, thus partly subject to and partly not within the council's jurisdiction. In short, another crazy Jerusalem story. Every once in a while one of our friends comes out to tell us what's happening. The two lawyers argue at length over the sentence, Lea striving hard to get the judge to impose a suspended punishment, conditional upon repeated offense. Eventually Ezra himself is given a chance to speak, and for once he holds back a little, following Lea's stern advice, though he lashes out at the Palestinian prosecutor for compromising what she must know to be the truth. The court adjourns. Sentencing will take place after a few weeks.

We pour outside into the molten summer sun. A small crowd has gathered to applaud Ezra and shake his hand. These are the stalwarts of the peace movement, or what's left of it: Jews and Palestinians, women and men, hardened by years in the field, by endless disappointments and trauma. We cluster around Ezra, the living heart of this struggle. There's not much we can do now except to wait and hope. In the meantime, there's work to be done in South Hebron. There's never an end to the work, and we long ago learned not to think too much about its fruits or, for that matter, its cost. I think we're all of us happy to take the risks.

October 24, 2009, Samu'a

"No settlers anywhere nearby, no soldiers, nothing will happen today"—Ezra keeps reassuring our Palestinian friends on the cell phone as we drive down to South Hebron in the early morning. By the time we reach our meeting point near Samu'a, a good group is in place: some twenty Palestinians and another eight or nine Ta'ayush activists. Most of the Palestinians belong to Samu'a, and the fields we are heading toward through the wadis belong to them, though they have no access to them any longer. The "illegal outpost" of Asa'el, one of the uglier and more malignant in this area, has grabbed them.

Ezra seems in good spirits despite the handing down of his sentence on Wednesday, three days ago. Judge Elata Ziskind, who had already found him guilty of assaulting two Border Policemen in February 2007, sentenced him to a month in jail, a fine of 750 Israeli shekels, another five hundred shekels to be paid to each of the allegedly traumatized policemen, and, the real killer, a six-month suspended jail sentence, in force for the next three years, to be activated any time Ezra is arrested again for "unlawful assembly" or similar heinous crimes. She clearly wanted to neutralize him for the coming years. In addition, she used the occasion to read out a moralistic sermon about orderliness and democracy. "Freedom of expression," she said, "is not the freedom to incite and take actions that prevent or disrupt police work . . . Democracy cannot allow this, for if the law enforcement system collapses, anarchy will reign and democracy and freedom of expression will be no more." It's more or less what one could have expected. But in fact, I think it's a classic document embodying not a legal but a moral failure of the first order.

Gandhi, as so often, stated the matter with excruciating clarity that day in 1922, when he addressed the court:

"The only course open to you, the Judge and the assessors, is either to resign your posts and thus dissociate yourselves from evil, if you feel that the law you are called upon to administer is an evil, and that in reality I am innocent, or to inflict on me the severest penalty, if you believe that the system and the law you are assisting to administer are good for the people of this country, and that my activity is, therefore, injurious to the common weal."

The judge, in reading out his judgment, implied that he had no choice but to send Gandhi to prison (for six years) for breaking the law, even though Gandhi had just outlined the very real choice that he did have. In my experience, people will generally prefer to believe themselves helpless rather than to assume the responsibility, and with it the agony, that inner freedom imparts. Whether Justice Ziskind felt any qualms or not is something we cannot know. What I, at least, do know is that the Israeli Occupation of Palestinian territories is a form of systemic wickedness, and it is that system that provides meaning to what Ezra did that day at Umm al-Khair.

Maybe the appeal will quash this verdict. The international

campaign clearly has had an effect. In the meantime, it's business as usual; it will take much more than this to stop Ezra Nawi.

So here we are in the sun-baked fields of Samu'a, in the mid-morning sun, just below Asa'el. I have to say these fields don't look too promising. There was little rain last year, and the land seems terminally dessicated, almost beyond redemption. My friend Eid, walking beside me, can see at a glance that even the thorny bushes they call *natj* have remained untouched for a long time by the goats who usually feed on them. Apparently, the settlers have driven the shepherds off. The few goat droppings he can see, with his farmer's eyes, are very old. The only fresh droppings are from the wild gazelles that roam these hills: recently Eid saw a herd of twenty of them, magnificent in these open spaces on the edge of the desert. To make these fields arable again, they will have to be cleared of stones and rained upon; the first task, a forbidding one, is ours. I glance over the first plot, at the bottom of the hill; at a conservative estimate, some ten thousand rocks, of varying shapes and sizes, will have to be pried out of the clay and reinstated as a terrace that will stand up to the water that will, hopefully, come pouring down the hill when the rains do start. By comparison, Sisyphus had an easy time.

We begin working with pickaxes and our bare hands, and as always there is the joy of doing it and especially of seeing the rightful owners of this land returning, at last, to care for it. I'm especially moved watching a middle-aged Palestinian woman working, face partly covered, hands heavy with thorns and stones, beside me. Of course we can't remove all the rocks, but the plot is looking more inviting by the minute, and soon we drift to the next terrace up, and the next one, getting closer at every step to the outer perimeter of the settlement on top of the hill. Naturally, we haven't gone unnoticed. A heavyset settler in his Shabbat white is staring down at us, and beside him there are soldiers, first only a few, then more and more, and in less than an hour, with the horrid sense of inevitability that so often signals human folly, they are clumsily descending in our direction. They are proudly waving the piece of paper that can only be the order declaring this area a Closed Military Zone.

The senior officer, bearded, young, opaque, reads it out: "By the authority legally vested in me, etc. etc." He gives us exactly ten minutes to desist from our subversive activity and to disappear. Well drilled in these rituals, we argue with him. If this is a CMZ and we are supposed to leave, we say, then why do those settlers on the hilltop get to stay? Ah yes, "by the authority vested in me, those whom I allow to stay can stay. You now have nine and a half minutes." Amiel leaps to the occasion. He carries with him, always, the text of the Supreme Court's ruling that local military commanders have no right to declare these closed military zones whenever the whim strikes them, and above all they are prohibited from using this mechanism to keep farmers away from their lands. Amiel reads out the text of the court's decision. The officer is utterly unimpressed. "You have eight minutes left."

We go back to work, and now each rock I pry from the recalcitrant soil seems to have some special meaning, as if defiance, however quixotic, were imprinted on it. The Palestinians also accelerate their pace. As always, the South Hebron hills are a good place for unexpected encounters. One of the soldiers, smiling, suddenly greets me by name. I don't recognize him at first, in his fancy-dress costume—helmet, uniform, rifle—but he tells me his name: Spartak, a former student. He studied Sanskrit with me, wrote a very good MA thesis. I haven't seen him for some years, but I announce at once to whoever wants to hear: "I don't mind being arrested, but only if Spartak carries out the order." It would be nice to hear his views on the task he is engaged in. "Seven and a half minutes." By now a genial policeman whom we know well from many such occasions has also turned up and announced, in his mild-mannered way, that by refusing to leave the CMZ we are committing a crime, hindering a public servant in discharging his duty (shades of Judge Ziskind). I figure this merits a response, so I say to him: "And what about those settlers? Their very presence here is a crime by international law and by any ethical standard." He smiles and nods. To my surprise, he agrees with me. "True," he says, "but that's not relevant now." "How could it not be relevant?" "Six minutes left before we start making arrests."

Now another blue-uniformed officer pipes up, offended by what we've been saying. "You're wrong. The settlers are pious people. I pray with them on Shabbat." "They're doing something terribly unjust to these innocent villagers," Amiel says. "Unjust?" says the policeman. "You want to talk about what is just? Leave justice to God. He knows what is just and unjust. You can't judge it. Compared to Him, you're like a worm." He says it not in a mean-hearted way, just stating the fact, for the record, and maybe to shore up his vision of the world just a little, the way we're trying to shore up the stone terraces. "That's just it," I say to him—I also care about the record— "I'm not a worm, and neither are you, and both of us are making choices every single minute, and I don't think God knows much better than you or me, for that matter. Look at the choice you're making right now." I wasn't planning on convincing him.

In the end it boils down to something relatively straightforward. The soldiers start by detaining three Palestinians: Kamal, 'Umar, and Mithat. We know Mithat—he's the one the settlers tied to a pole and beat to within an inch of his life, not that long ago. Amiel arrived on the scene and found him, badly injured, still shackled to the pole. Anyway, there's no way we can let the Palestinians get carted off to jail alone, so Amiel demands to be detained with them, and we're not about to let Amiel go alone, so Yehuda and Tamar and Amit and I gather up our things and join him. For Amit and Tamar, it's the first time. There's always the first time. It's a gentle enough arrest; there's no violence involved apart from the rampant collective violence implicit in every word the soldiers have said today and in their presence here beside the settlers who are now photographing us, one by one, again for the record—though it's Shabbat, and the law they supposedly honor prohibits taking pictures on this day.

We sit in the airless, ugly vehicle in which arrestees are transported. Midday: dusty and hot. We settle in; we introduce ourselves. 'Umar, with a grand mustache and immense, natural dignity, is an officer in the Palestinian security forces (this doesn't give him any immunity from Israeli military law). The fields we were clearing belong to his family. Mithat, wiry and voluble, is a teacher. Amit, a mathematician and philosopher, has been studying Greek in Tel Aviv, and suddenly I remember that I have a volume of Homer, in the original, in my bag. We'll have plenty of time to read some together at the station, I promise him. He can't wait. He wants to start right now. So you can imagine us sitting on the beat-up, springless seats of the armored car, waiting to move, a little thirsty, waiting for it all to begin again so that eventually it will be over, but meanwhile slowly reading the hexameters: "The Achaians, remembering the day glorious Hektor raged there, came spilling out over the plain, and now Hera cast a heavy fog around the Trojans, to block their way. . . ."

It's a long ride. The half-track drives with excruciating

sluggishness. We leave Asa'el, descend to the main road, crawl
pass the turn-offs to Susya and Twaneh and Deirat, eventually
wind our way through the vast settler-city of Kiryat Arba. They
bring us in to the police station. As it happens, Amiel spent
most of yesterday in this same waiting room; he was arrested
when Ta'ayush activists erected a Palestinian "outpost," on Palestinian land, in protest at the endless series of Israeli outposts
that keep going up all over the territories and that usually turn
into permanent Israeli settlements. The Ta'ayush outpost was
torn down by the army within half an hour. Amiel is at home in
the Kiryat Arba station, and the policemen seem to honor him.
One of them says to me in what must be police-speak: "If you
were to take the DNA of an ordinary policeman and graft some
of Amiel's DNA onto it, you'd get a real Super-Policeman."

So here's another extended, even picaresque moment in this
endless day of futile gestures and the mad, intimate comraderie
of Israelis in and out of the Occupation. There's certainly no
one here to be angry at. We're told that one of the settlers who
wanted to submit a complaint against us decided to go all the
way to the Beer-Sheva station, far to the south, because "the
Kiryat Arba station is manned by leftists." I guess it's all relative. In any case, the ritual is played out, with eerie grace, to the
end. Each of us has to be interrogated, most of us holding fast
to our right to remain silent—except for Amiel, who wants the
Supreme Court ruling to be written into his interrogation sheet
in case a judge ever gets to read it. My interrogator, Yoram, is
respectful and bemused. He tells me I am charged with entering into a forbidden area and with obstructing a public servant
in the exercise of his duty; I think there's also another item
about obstructing someone else from doing something else.
Every once in a while he asks me: "Why won't you answer my

questions?" I explain the logic to him. In exchange he offers me a little good-natured grumbling: "One day it's you, the next day it's the settlers, the day after that the Palestinians. You never get any rest around here." Since it's Shabbat, he also has to do everything by himself, including the awkward business of taking my fingerprints and palm-prints and photographs. It takes a while. Seven or eight hours go by, with a few more hexameters for comfort, until they finally call us in, in pairs, to tell us that we are being ordered out of South Hebron for the next eight days. We sign the forms and are released into the fragrant night with its waxing moon. All this because we were trying to clear a few fields of rocks?

And then you remember. You remember Ezra, who has been sentenced to jail because he stood up to protect the innocent from something both monstrous and routine. You remember the Palestinian woman scraping at those stones in her ravished field. You remember that the policemen and the soldiers and the judge are all part of this monstrous thing, and you can see how most of them have long ago decided to let God decide what's right or wrong—anything so as not to have to make the choice themselves. There are moments you could weep that human beings could be like this. You remember what Priam said to Achilles, how he kissed the hand that had killed his son, and how the two of them wept together, Achilles remembering his old father, and how the whole huge war and everything that had been said or sung about it suddenly seemed so futile and foolish and unbearable, a world empty of anything remotely like glory but suffused by shame. You remember how you didn't really want to get up so early this morning and go off to South Hebron because it all seems so futile, and now that today is over it still feels futile and yet strangely beautiful, as if some intimate chord had been struck even if no one could hear it. Maybe, you might think for a passing moment, it's beautiful *because* it's futile—but actually you don't believe that.

I think back to how the day began, when we were driving south with Ezra and suddenly there were ragged children playing ball by the roadside; the ball rolled onto the highway, and Ezra stopped the car right there in the middle of the vast desert and waited for them to cross over and retrieve their ball safely, and I thought: it's a small, everyday gesture, hardly worth noticing in the midst of the madness, but this is the act of a good man.

August 6, 2011, Al-Ganub and Al-Sa'ir

I knew it was a mistake as soon as I said it.

I was apologizing to Russil—an activist guest from abroad, first time in South Hebron—about the relatively placid hours we'd spent here in Ganub. I thought she'd like to see some action, the standard Ta'ayush fare. Maybe it was even a little boring? "Boring?" says one of the Palestinians. "You know," I say, teasing him, "no settlers, no police, no soldiers. . . ." "This is how we like it," he says, and I have to agree. We've had long hours talking quietly in the shade with new friends.

Hardly are the words out of my mouth than the first jeep of soldiers comes crawling down the road.

We came to help them fix the road, which is full of potholes, rocks, and bumps. But they didn't really need us to do the work. Heavy dump trucks unloaded piles of gravel and sand, and eventually, around noon, a yellow tractor turned up to roll these piles over the road and press them into the hard surface and smooth it all down. It was a struggle to get the tractor to come, since the owner was afraid that if something went wrong and the army showed up, the soldiers would confiscate the priceless tractor. Husain persuaded the owner to take the risk and stood surety for the tractor's safe return.

It's Ramadan, and our hosts are fasting. They keep telling us that we can drink and eat, that we *must* drink in this heat, and midmorning they bring us hot sweet tea that I don't really want to consume. "If you're fasting," I say to Muhammad, "I'm fasting with you," but he brusquely refuses even to consider this gesture of solidarity: I have to drink the tea. It is all we can do to dissuade them from preparing us a huge midday meal. We promise to come back for the festival, 'Id, when the month of fasting ends.

They are tough, weather-beaten farmers and shepherds, most of them from the village of Sa'ir, which means "Blazing Fire" or even "Hellfire"—a strange name for a village, which they explain by telling us that long ago this was a wild region, infested by bandits who preyed on the caravans moving between Syria and the Hijaz. Their more recent story is the usual one in the territories. First they lost thousands of acres to the settlements of Metzad, beginning in the early 1980s. Then they suffered through the years of indignity: the time settlers set fire to two houses, thus burning up the thousands of Jordanian dinars that were kept there; the sight of an ancient well that has been made into a settlers' swimming pool; the periodic attacks and insults, an endless epic of injustice. Still, I think to myself, listening to Muhammad, with his deep, deliberate voice, that by South Hebron standards they've got off not so badly. No one killed. They also had one unusual success in the courts, which forced the dismissal of the last security officer in the nearby settlement, a very violent man by their account. But these are people who know about racism, and the bitter word, *'unsuriya,* comes readily off their tongues: "Are we not, you and I, both creatures born after nine months? So why do *they* have water and electricity and we have none? We were born here, in the caves on these hills, but *they* came from outside and told us, 'Go away, you don't belong here.' Who are they to tell me I don't belong? Still, the settlers know they are doing wrong. I go out on the hills with my sheep, I put my head down to sleep wherever I like, I'm not afraid, but they build fences around themselves, and watchtowers, and they bring watchdogs and guns to protect themselves. It is the criminal who is afraid."

He offers something like a proverb. "There is the person who sees you in pain and who feels your pain with you, and there is the person who sees you burning and adds wood to the fire." So one thing, at least, I can say about myself and about every one of the volunteers who came down today: We feel the pain. In fact, my whole body aches with it, a sharp hurt that sits inside me, waits for me when I wake, taunts me day by day. Why have I not done more?

Muhammad has two wives. He wanted to build a small room for the second wife, maybe with a bathroom, attached to his home, but the Civil Administration, of course, wouldn't let him do it.

Many of the men have spent long years in Israeli prisons. Here is Husain, first arrested at the age of seventeen, imprisoned for fourteen years: "I was a soldier fighting for the land. Now I've changed. Today I'm a soldier for peace. I believe we will reach peace and a Palestinian state with east Jerusalem as its capital. It's an honest hope, and I have earned the right to feel hope."

Again and again they tell us: "We don't want you to work today, it is enough that you are here with us." But maybe we can after all be of use. Just two weeks ago settlers fenced off another large field that belongs to these families and have already plowed it. I think we'll get it back.

Now, just when it seems the day is ending, as the tractor advances to the other side of the ridge and can no longer be seen, and I am joking about boredom, just now the soldiers come.

They head straight for the tractor with us right beside them. We quickly realize that a heinous crime has been committed: Palestinians have had the temerity to work on a winding, bumpy dirt road that runs on their own land—*without asking permission.* How dare they? So the soldiers have come to stop them and make them pay. The tractor driver is clearly scared. They take away his identity card, they threaten him, they call their superiors on their cell phones. We wait. After a while they tell him to get into the tractor and drive away, fast.

So the first, acute danger has passed. They didn't arrest him and didn't impound the tractor. Relief. But by now more soldiers are flooding in through the trees, a steady stream; six vehicles pull up, senior officers get out, and then two police vans arrive, a bad sign. They take Husain's identity card, and Danny's and Dolev's. Stating the obvious, a tall lieutenant from the Civil Administration says to Husain: "You can't just decide to fix this road."

"But it's our own road, on our land, we can prove it to you, even your own courts have acknowledged this."

"Maybe it is, maybe it isn't, I don't care, but you didn't ask for a permit."

"And would you have given me a permit? Look, arrest me if you want. I'm not afraid, and I'll take responsibility for what we did."

"I don't need to arrest you. I'll call you in the morning. Meanwhile, don't touch the road. Leave everything as it is."

"But *we* brought these piles of gravel, and now the road is blocked, and we need to use it."

"Don't touch them. I will call you in the morning and we'll straighten it all out."

He says it maybe six times. Tomorrow he will telephone—a mild threat. Who knows what they'll think up by then? But he's a reasonable man. He's also part of the system, and the system tells him that you have to show them who's in control. Anyone can see what will happen if you let them fix their own road on their own initiative. The next thing you know, there will be suicide bombers in the cities, and then missiles from Lebanon and Syria, and probably a catastrophic war, the end of the State of Israel, the final demise of the Jewish people, the Jewish God will have a bad day, and all this because of one dusty road and three heaps of gravel that the tractor didn't have time to spread out evenly. If you allow them even an infinitesimal taste of freedom, the whole fabric of your life will unravel. They live at your discretion, and they must learn this time after time.

Anyway, that's how I try to explain it to Russil, who's a bit shocked at this sudden massive invasion. But actually I think it's something much deeper that's happening, something resistant to normal thought. We could maybe explain it by the basic fact of the land grab, the settlement enterprise that determines everything the army does in the territories and requires dispossession and harassment of Palestinians whenever possible. But beyond that is refined, half-conscious hate that fuels the endless rules and whims of the system, that revels in cruelty. Lunacy is remorseless; it must play itself out in recurrent minidramas like this one, a seemingly trivial case in which everyone, including us, must memorize their lines and play their part.

As so often before, I contemplate the rampant madness with its ironic intimacies. Just look at it—the soldiers, black machine guns, camouflage helmets, heavy ammunition belts, combat boots; the policemen with their nametags and their air of weary impatience; the Palestinians milling aimlessly around, all too familiar with such moments; the Ta'ayush activists, filming furiously; the afternoon sun baking all of us; the disembodied words that the soldiers speak, words with no evident meaning except to hurt and to claim power. And meanwhile the white gravel is cooking on the unfinished road, and on the hill in the distance shepherds are grazing their black goats; I see them trickling down over the burning rocks like flecks of ebony, the loveliest sight I've ever seen.

The thing is, the absurdity actually feels real and utterly compelling, in fact more real in its craziness than the rather orderly life that I live in Jerusalem, so that in the end I am no longer sure which of these two realities is the more ridiculous.

After an hour, maybe more, the soldiers leave, except for one jeep that is supposed to watch us from the distance. But what about the road, still blocked by three piles of sand and gravel? We clear them away with buckets and shovels and our bare hands and our feet, and as always, these minutes of simple physical labor are the best moments of my day, and then the soldiers come back because we have done what they expressly forbade us to do, we have touched the road. And again there are threats, and by now the Palestinians are angry, unable to bear even one more insult, but we have more or less flattened out the piles so that cars can pass again, and after much going back and forth between the soldiers and our friends it is agreed that the army will go and we will go and no one will be arrested today, for a change. We take our leave from Husain and Muhammad and 'Abd al-Rahim and the others, we thank them, we promise to return.

Still, they're unhappy because they haven't fed us, though

they're still some hours away from breaking their fast, so before we go they rush into the almond grove and poke at the trees with long poles so that the green almonds fall to the ground. They are huge, and actually not only green but also a subtle pink-purple-brown, like gradations of peach or mango, with the hard shell of the nut inside this outer casing. The farmers gather them up in a bucket that they bring to our minibus, and one man has folded some almonds into his shirt and shakes them out, dozens of them, on the front seat beside Yihya the driver, and that is how we drive away in the sunlight—awash in unripe almonds.

September 15, 2012, Gawawis and Khala'il al-Khair

I've never been expelled from my home or my lands or from anywhere else. No doubt my ancestors could have said something about it. When I came to live in Israel some forty-five years ago, I never dreamed that someday I'd be spending my weekends trying to keep Palestinian farmers and shepherds from suffering that prototypically Jewish trauma—at the hands of the Jews.

It feels like hell, even if you're just watching it happen to someone else. There are times when I think I can't go through it again. I'm walking beside the shepherds and the goats, and behind me the soldiers and border policemen are barking orders, telling me to move on, telling me that I'm still inside the Closed Military Zone that they've drawn in blue on their army maps that, under duress, they finally let us see. Today the soldiers were particularly bad. The battalion commander is young, supercilious, arrogant. He loves saying things like, "You don't know anything about this, and anyway fifteen seconds have already gone by, which leaves four minutes and forty-five seconds before we arrest you." He keeps looking at his watch, especially when Amiel explains to him, with cool clarity, that what he, the battalion commander, is doing is totally illegal.

The battalion commander, who refuses to divulge his name, turned up right from the start, around 7:30 in this almost-autumnal morning. A minute before a deer had raced past us with that wild grace that human beings are mostly incapable of achieving. Instead of those arcs and leaps, we use words, mostly to no great effect. The hills were almost blue in the early morning, the sheep were grazing with gusto, and the shepherds were clearly happy to be back on this thorny hill that is theirs, of course, for centuries but to which they normally have no access. The settlement of Mitzpeh Yair sits on top of the hill, and two settlers in their white Shabbat clothes have already come down to harass us, with the soldiers fast on their heels.

I'm used to all gradations of human wickedness in the South Hebron hills, but the battalion commander easily ranks among the worst I've seen in recent years. On second thought, I suppose the settlers who have attacked us from time to time, with murder in their eyes, might rank even lower. But the battalion commander, let's not forget, has the power. He is the public face of the Occupation. He literally calls the shots. He has a long black submachine gun, as do all of his men, and he seems to enjoy fondling it as he forces us downhill. At one point Amiel says to Maria, who is protesting at this abuse of authority and the blatant contravention of the army's own laws: "There is the law, and they're violating it at every level, but here the law doesn't really exist. The only law that counts is this gun." He draws a long ellipse with his hand in the space inhabited by the gun, which in fact hides nearly all of the battalion commander's short body. The man has become his gun. I know it can happen; I remember from the war.

He interests me, the battalion commander, and I wish I

could draw him into conversation; but this is almost impossible. He is reveling in his power to push us out of his lordly domain. Still, I figure I have to try. "Don't you feel a little bad inside yourself?" I say to him.

"No."

Of course we have recited to him the Supreme Court rulings about Closed Military Zones, about how the army is strictly forbidden to impose one on Palestinian grazing grounds or fields if this means keeping the farmers and shepherds off their lands, about how the commander in the field is required to show us the order and the attached map and to allow us to photograph them, about arbitrary arrest and arbitrary rulings and all the other things that are standard practice here in the Wild South. None of this has made the slightest impression. The battalion commander, still looking at his watch, has been joined by a senior commander from the Civil Administration and another one from the Border Police, bearded and black, whom I remember from previous encounters.

In the end, he's the one who detains Ella and me. It happens like this. We were prepared to defy the order and the Closed Military Zone and get arrested on the top of the hill, but the shepherds, at the last minute, decided not to risk arrest, which is potentially a big thing for them and can last for a long time. There are two of them—a father and his son—and the father, sun-beaten, beaten down in other ways too, shrugs and says, "We'll go water the goats." The well is some ways down the hill, in the direction the soldiers want us to go. We have our rule: if our Palestinian hosts back off, we won't try to make them stay and fight it out. Once they go, there's no point in our staying. So very slowly and deliberately, at the pace of a stubborn goat, with the soldiers bullying and threatening from behind, dogging our steps, we begin our descent.

My spirits sink. At the bottom of my stomach, black bile thickens and boils. I hate this. Unusually for me, I even hate the battalion commander. I feel insulted in every inch of my body. He treats the Palestinians with contempt and us with virulent disgust. Words like "law" or "decency" clearly mean nothing to him. Maybe words in general mean little to him. I feel impotent. I can't protect these innocent shepherds, can't break through the crystal surface of human cruelty. I want to see the battalion commander in the prisoner's dock at the Hague. Maybe someday he'll be there, and I'll come and remind him of this morning in South Hebron. I'll bear witness against him, since I promise you I will never forget. Even better would be if this narrow, clenched, hard-hearted man would somehow, later in his life, by some miracle, become a human being. I think there's a chance.

But the worst of it is that feeling of losing what is most yours. I figure the shepherds must be feeling it. Maybe even the goats somehow sense it. These thorns and rocks are your friends, you have spent your childhood and youth among them, and then the settlers arrived and with them the soldiers and the officious clerks of the Civil Administration waving their papers and they all said you have no right to be here any longer and drove you away at gunpoint. And today you came back until they drove you away again, and we couldn't help.

Of course, this isn't the end of the story. Our lawyers will work on the case, and we'll go to court if we have to, and in the end these shepherds will have the right to graze here unhindered. Usually, if we persist, that's how it ends. We have filmed it all, the courts will have no dearth of evidence, the result is more or less known in advance. We've been through it many times. But for the moment, as the sun rages higher in the sky, I rage, too.

Then they make a mistake. They seem suddenly to realize that Nasser, our close friend from Susya, is a Palestinian, thus vulnerable to their threats. He's been walking with us downhill toward the road that constitutes the outer border of the CMZ, but they stop him and demand that he hand over his identity card. "You don't belong here," says the Border Policeman, studying the card. "You're not allowed to be in this zone." He's detained. So now there's no question about what we have to do. We turn around. The older shepherd is hauling buckets of water from the well for the goats. We stand beside him, facing the bullies and their guns. Amiel, furious, says to the battalion commander: "Everything you've done today was illegal, but now what you're doing is racist, in more ways than one, and I won't allow it to happen." Arresting the Palestinian and allowing the Jews to go free—there's no way we'll accept this. As they begin to drag Nasser back up the hill, where Nissim, veteran photographer of these expeditions, has already been detained, we follow them. The Border Policeman turns to Ella and me and says: "Stop. Where do you think you're going?"

"We're going with Nasser."

"Give me your identity cards. You're being detained."

Amiel, Dolev, and several others have suffered the same fate. We march uphill. I'm feeling better already. In fact, a wave of relief washes over me. The world suddenly looks more interesting. It's only a small, an infinitesimal act of defiance and resistance, but it's enough to make you feel alive again. Black bile begins to dissolve. Life offers you a chance from time to time. You can do the right thing. The initiative has suddenly, surprisingly, passed to us. The battalion commander looks far from pleased, though I hear him say to one of his officers, "Don't worry, this is good for us." He's probably glad to see us arrested, though he enjoyed driving us off even more. Lately, when the soldiers arrest us because of Closed Military Zones, they usually tack on another, entirely invented charge, like "attacking an officer" or "preventing a policeman from discharging his duties" or "illegal assembly." What this means, in practice, is that the legal procedures drag on and may go to court and may end with a ban on entering South Hebron for some weeks or months—or worse, much worse, if they can make the fake charges stick.

We climb the hill. Eventually they group us together near the main road. We wait, as one always waits in such situations. It's hot. To add to my joy, we hear the messages coming through on the police network. They have phoned in our identity numbers, and someone sitting near a computer in some air-conditioned office far away has checked them and calls back with what she's discovered: "David Shulman, *takin*. [That is: OK, acceptable, in good working order]." "Ella Janatovsky— *tekina*." We burst out laughing. I say to the policeman: "I don't think my wife would agree." Ella sends a Facebook message: "The police say I'm OK!"

A black-uniformed super-policeman turns up, a welcome antidote to the battalion commander. Young, genial, assuming control, the policeman beams at us and says, all butter and honey: "Just in case you have a feeling that the police are anti-leftist, I want you to know that this is simply not the case. We aren't pro or anti anybody. We're here to enforce the law." Ezra, standing beside him, nods and says, "Of course. God forbid you should be partisan." "No, really," says the policeman, "I mean it. We're completely neutral." "I would never doubt it," says Ezra. This goes on for a while. Slowly it dawns on me that we won't be spending the next few hours in the police station after all.

They return our identity cards. Nasser, Amiel, and Dolev have to fill out "detention forms." Then they, too, will be released. I hope the battalion commander is eating his heart.

We go with Ezra to Bi'r al-'Id for a double visit. First there is tea with Haj Isma'il. Recently four settlers attacked him with iron bars and knives; he had to be hospitalized. Today he's looking more or less all right, except for one hand where you can still see the scars from the slashes and two bad spots on his skull. His skin has the texture of rock. "You'll be fine in time for the wedding," Ezra teases him. Haj Isma'il has four wives and thirty-three children, but he's been trying for years to persuade the Qadi to allow him to marry a fifth.

"We've seen it all," he says to us. "The Turks, the British, and the Jordanians all ruled us, but we've seen nothing as bad as the Israelis, *ma shufna as'ab min Israel.*"

Then there's another donkey. Ezra found him abandoned on the road, very weak, thin, sick. He adopted him. Now he brings him delicacies to eat every time he comes (which is most days). The donkey has discriminating tastes. He is particularly fond of ripe grapes and rice cakes. We offer him some of both along with a few south Indian cashews. He still looks a little skinny, his white hair thinned out and scraggly. "You love donkeys," I say to Ezra, mindful of similar visits long ago. "It's not that I love them," Ezra says, "but I feel sorry for them. Everyone is always making fun of them and exploiting them without mercy. They're sturdy and reliable and no prima donnas. They deserve to live, too."

3

ON WICKEDNESS

I prefer to speak of wickedness rather than of evil, and that is because the former has, I think, a more personal ring to it and makes it a little easier to think about whether a person might have some room for making a personal decision when wickedness rises up in him or her. To my ear "evil" sounds abstract, even disembodied, and that makes for a false start, as if we were dealing with some autonomous preexistent force or power or attribute of reality itself, or of the mind—whereas most of the wickedness I have known seems always to come from complex, whole human beings who are not so easily split into bodies and minds, or into dark and luminous parts of their selves. I have seen much wickedness over the years, and not only in the South Hebron hills; but I think it's relatively rare to find a thoroughly wicked person. In fact, in my life as a whole I have met only one person who was, by nature, so treacherous and vicious, and so radically oblivious to others' suffering, so completely immune to even the possibility of sorrow or remorse, that he could be called profoundly wicked, beyond redemption. I am sure that there are many other such people, but he's the only one I've known.

I assume there is wickedness to some degree in each of us, and there is definitely such a thing as collective wickedness that envelops everyone it touches. The Israeli Occupation of Palestine is a hothouse of wickedness of varying intensities, from the almost negligible to the truly inhuman. Terrible in its overall character, in its insult to human dignity on a mass scale, it generates terrible deeds in nearly all who hold power. But wait: perhaps wickedness as such can never be negligible. Each moment of humiliation, or theft, or physical violence, or arbitrary punishment, or premeditated terror, is singular and consequential.

I want to explore this business of wickedness and its habitual manifestation in inflicting cruelty, deliberately or not. These are of interest not in a theoretical sense but in lived experience, in the fiercely sensual and tangible reality of the Occupation. Perhaps wickedness in general holds a gloomy attraction for human beings (this might explain Israeli voting habits over the last several decades). I am interested in the ways cruelty emerges, actively or passively, in the individual who has power.

Let us put aside the straightforward, simple ways of the bully. They require little explanation. It is May 2013. A settler from Otniel comes charging into the grazing grounds of Palestinian Umm al-'Amad (actually, all of Otniel sits on land taken from Umm al-'Amad and other nearby villages). This settler does his best to drive the sheep and goats away; mostly silent, callous, brutal, he strides over the hill, his face set in a hard mask, his features limned with hate. To the shepherds he says, actually screams, several times: "I'll get you fucked." Other than that, he says nothing. He is, of course, heavily armed. I saw him and heard him. I don't want to say more about him. He is one case among many. There is nothing very interesting here. He inhabits a world where what he did that day is so ordinary, so entirely natural, that it elicits no special notice—not on the part of his settler colleagues, and not in the eyes of the soldiers or the police, who in any case almost always collude with him in such acts. Only the shepherds pay some attention to his insults. Don't misunderstand: I don't think this close-to-innocuous act of bullying is in any sense banal. No evil act is banal. Nor do I find the evildoer banal, though that doesn't make him interesting.

Of course, there are endless incidents that are far worse and that are also at least as ordinary and routine as the one I've just mentioned. What can one say about the three settlers who tied Mithat to a pole somewhere out in the open hills and then beat him almost to death?[2] I suppose these settlers enjoyed beating Mithat, and they no doubt had some thought in their minds that helped them rationalize what they were doing, since human beings seem always to need such thoughts.

The Policeman

Let us take a more complex and engaging case. Perhaps you still remember the policeman who arrested several of us at Samu'a on October 24, 2009.[3] I'll call him S. I've known him for quite some time. I like him. He apparently also used to like me. Occasionally, when we would meet in the field, he would say, "Ah, Professor Shulman—it's been a while since you've been my guest." He's a friendly guy, with a twinkle in his eye. More important, he sometimes intimates that he shares our political views, more or less. On more than one occasion I have said to him something like: "Look at what you're doing here. You are in the presence of the rightful owners and of the thieves who have taken their land, and you're aiding and abetting the thieves." To which he would reply something like: "You may be right, but I'm here to enforce the law."

When he says such things, and acts upon what he has said, I can, I think, see something, however limited, of what is going on in his mind. He is *not* a person lacking conscience. Unlike nearly all Israelis, he is not turning away. I sense in him at such moments a conflict transpiring inside in complicated ways. Not everything needs to be conscious. Probably things happen very fast.

Of course, I don't really know what is happening in his mind or heart. I don't even know what is happening in mine. But I hear the music of his voice, somehow dissonant with the words. I see his eyes.

It goes without saying that this is no laboratory experiment under sterile conditions. I can't isolate one element from another. The Indians would say that his thinking at such a moment is profoundly conditioned by every previous thought he has had and everything he has ever done. Not *determined* but conditioned or constrained. This person, like all others, has been creating himself and his future at every moment in his life—not freely, perhaps, but nonetheless shaping the person he is and will be. So could he suddenly stop and not think or do what he has thought and done in the past? Yes, in theory he could.

But at what point would he do so? Here is the South Hebron version of Zeno's paradox. It is, says Zeno, impossible for us to traverse any defined distance or space, say a room, because the remaining space to the end of the room can always be divided into two or more, and we can never cross these infinite divisions. S. has been flowing along in the rushing course of his life, with its certainties and its ambiguities and its zones of relative security, and this progression has involved what I am calling wickedness at many instants. There is no point in the river at which S. can truly cross to the other side—at which he could say, for example, "no." Such a "no" is not a *point.*

And yet I am confident that whatever else is passing through his mind at these moments, there is something that can only be called a choice. I can't say anything about his express intentions. He doesn't sit in meditative silence, weigh the options, and decide. Nothing like that. He is not even aware of making the choice. But I, from the outside, can see him make it. I have watched him do so several times. It is, I think, a very subtle moment, one that could, again in theory, go either way, though in practice it always goes only in one way, the wrong one in my view. S. chooses to do something wicked, something that causes pain to innocent people, something they experience as cruel. I think he makes this choice as a whole person, indeed the choice expresses the wholeness, as well as the singularity, of who he is, though this totality of the person may well include whole chunks that are mildly dissociated, that cannot quite feel or imagine the suffering to which he is contributing. Indeed, the interplay of dissociation and various measures of awareness may well be what constitutes the totality and holds it together.

But let's not overdo this conclusion about choice. It's not as if he's in any kind of agony about it, at least not as far as he knows. It's always possible that the bad choice eats away at him somewhere inside and that he pays a price, without realizing it. I think we probably always pay for suppressing our natural identification with another person's pain. I also think that this idea, very close to Buddhist notions of karma, is on the verge of the romantic. In practice, as a glance outside will disclose, the wicked mostly flourish like the green bay tree.

But S., let me remind you, is not really wicked. He has wicked moments. He has them consistently and repeatedly. On the whole, however, S. is a good man. There's no hint of taking pleasure at another's pain. Still, he chooses to do his part in inflicting pain. It's important to remember that he is not alone in the field when the choice takes place. He's surrounded by soldiers and other policemen and settlers, all of them urging him to choose what anyway he wants to choose and, indeed, in a sense cannot but choose, except for that very subtle margin where I can see him waver slightly, very slightly. How could he extricate himself from the web of loyalties that define his place in the world? "What looks like power is, in fact, something that is extremely dependent upon the audience shouting support."[4]

What are the chances that S. would ever act differently, say on some hypothetical day when the cruelty was simply too blatant for him to deal with? To answer this question one needs to assume a probabilistic universe. I'm reluctant to assume this a priori. There are cases of people like S. who did choose differently, like the soldier at Bil'in I mentioned earlier.[5] So why not S.?

I know very well why not. Again I have to say that we are dealing with very subtle, internal processes, opaque for the most part to the subject himself. Still, I am impressed by the Hindu philosophical claim that some very trivial factor may well be enough to cure a person of his or her recalcitrant ignorance of truth. Why is that? Because knowledge of truth, which includes the potential for goodness, is, they say, the most intimate kind of knowledge, something we know even before we know that we know it, something given to human beings with life itself. Ignorance, they say, is like balancing a fruit on your nose; the slightest breeze or movement of the head is enough to make it fall away.[6]

Sadly, this rather hopeful view of human awareness must contend with the empirical observation that our relations with wickedness and cruelty are no less intimate, and possibly no less opaque. Let the reader ask herself, as I ask myself, if the idea of inflicting pain on another—or even the occasional wish to do so—is alien to her awareness. It's certainly not alien to mine. We might ask ourselves whether introspective knowledge of this kind—knowledge, that is, of incipient wickedness as such—is present in the awareness of a person who is actively inflicting pain. Socrates thought it could not be—that is, he thought that knowing something is evil and/or harmful to oneself and then doing it was a psychological impossibility. I wish I could agree with him.

But what about the systemic framing of this situation on a hot morning in the fields of Samuʻa? S. is definitely part of a ramified system that makes it both possible and necessary for him to choose the wicked. This system is external to S. and was in place even before he was born, though he has surely taken large parts of it into himself. I am sympathetic to this notion of system. Nearly everyone who finds himself or herself inside such a system goes along with it most, if not all, of the time. I understand how difficult, indeed mostly impossible, it is to extricate yourself from the system, which can always crush you without effort. The systemic view erases the humanistic one, in which the possibility of choice survives even if the acting subject lacks the inner freedom to make the choice. Yet not all such systems are equivalent, or equally encompassing. Modern nationalism tends to generate systemic oppression, to swallow up the free individual, sacrificing him or her to some false god. The drive toward the systemic, Nietzsche said, is always a matter of bad faith.

I guess we've had enough of S. Now that I've looked again at the story, trying to explain it to myself and to you, I feel weary and dispirited. I could be altogether wrong about S. Perhaps he's far more hard-hearted than he seems. Perhaps there are very large dead zones inside him where he simply does not, indeed cannot, feel. Perhaps he can only feel the approbation of his colleagues in the audience.

No. I don't think that is the case.

Settlers

The Occupation system has a cutting edge. Take the term literally. It has a name.

Routinely, we encounter violent settlers in the field. I have seen not a few who are overtly sadistic, as in the example I cited at the start of this chapter. All Palestinians living in Area C, where nearly all the settlements have been placed, have experienced settler violence. Moreover, the very presence of these settlements on Palestinian land constitutes a stark instance of state terror; the enterprise as a whole is saturated with wickedness.

But that doesn't mean that all settlers are alike, or that they can collectively be classed as wicked. Like any large group— and there are now several hundred thousand settlers in the occupied territories—they are heterogeneous, with a range of views and feelings. It's important for me to state this clearly. Some years ago, after the publication of *Dark Hope* in Hebrew, a group of young settlers, leaders of youth groups, called me and asked that we meet. I was hesitant. Over the phone I asked them if they were sure they wanted to meet me: "After all," I said, "I think that all of you are part of a vast criminal scheme." Yes, they said, they very much wanted to meet. Partly against my better judgment, I agreed. My son helped me prepare myself internally. "Just remember," he said, "they are mostly good people who happen to be mistaken."

We met on a hot summer afternoon on the roof of the Museum on the Seam—the historic boundary between western (Israeli) Jerusalem and the eastern, Palestinian sections of the city. We had a long, impassioned, painful talk, holding nothing back. I quickly saw that they represented a range of viewpoints—from those on the extreme right who wanted to load all Palestinians onto trucks and dump them on the other side of the border to a few more or less moderate voices not without inner conflict. One theme that kept coming up, on their side, was the overriding value that lies in the Jews' sticking together, despite differences of opinion: solidarity before all. Clearly, there was no way I could accept this.

When the session was over, they followed the time-honored tradition in Israeli youth movements of asking each participant to say what he or she had taken away from the meeting. One of the settlers said that if he met me at a demonstration, he wouldn't spit at me. I regarded this as a meaningful achievement. Another said that it was impressive to find a person as old as I was still committed to idealistic action, albeit it, unfortunately, in an utterly wrong-headed cause. Another said he now hated me a little less than before the talk. One relatively more open settler admitted to feeling confused.

As for me, I learned something important. They explained that they had asked to meet me because, in my book, I had tended to lump all settlers together with the savage ones who so often had assaulted us on the hills of South Hebron. They insisted on the critical differences that clearly obtained among those present, to say nothing of the much wider settler circles. I saw that they were right.

So for the record let me say that over the years I have met

settlers who are gentle people, capable of argument, sometimes (rarely) even able to hear our vision of what is right and
what is wrong. They tend, however, to be thoroughly imbued
with the fierce ideology of the religious right, which is mostly
immune to claims based on universal values. Recently, in the
Jordan Valley, we encountered a group of four young settlers—
hardly more than teenagers—who were undeniably involved
in acts of wanton brutality directed against the Bedouin shepherds whose lands they had stolen. We spoke with them for
some time, at their initiatve. At some point one of them said
to us: "What you are saying is correct from a human point of
view. We are behaving with great cruelty toward these people.
It's not just that I don't want them to graze their herds here, on
this hill. I don't want them to be on this hill at all, or anywhere
nearby, on *any* hill. I want them to go away, to not be here, and
that's not very nice. However, if you believe the word of the
Bible, you know that God gave this land to the Jews—*only* to
us. All that we do follows inevitably from that." Human beings
usually need a modicum of rationalization to make sense of the
wicked things they do. This need may be one of the defining
features of our species.

Do these settlers have a choice? Yes, without doubt. Moreover, for most of them the choice excludes the very possibility
of doubt on their part. Even worse, as a collective they tend
to condone acts of violence committed by members of their
own community, or to condemn such acts half-heartedly, as
tolerable aberrations from a higher norm. Sadly, anyone who
knows the reality in the territories knows that settler violence
is intrinsic to the Occupation system, and that it is actively
exploited as such by Israeli governments in pursuit of their
greater annexationist goal. Highly nontrivial wickedness exists
at all levels of the system. As a result, innocents suffer every
hour, and many die.

The Bureaucrats

After the sociopathic settlers, by far the worst, in my experience, are the officers and bureaucrats of the Civil Administration—that is, the formal apparatus of the Occupation, a unit of the Israeli army. These senior bureaucrats are not, of course, all cut from the same cloth. I've met in the field—rarely, I have to say—CA officers who are honest, humane men. Occasionally, one of them has intervened in a situation pregnant with cruelty in a way that defused the torment. For example, there was the time when we were plowing a field bordering on the "illegal" settlement of Asa'el (as it is classed under Israeli law, though it is no more illegal than all the others), and the settlers came out to stop us, and the soldiers turned up and put a halt to the work. Things were stuck for an hour or two while the settlers screamed curses and urged the soldiers to shoot us on the spot. Eventually a senior Druze officer[7] of the CA arrived and, for once, ordered the soldiers to protect the Palestinian farmers as they completed their work. This officer, incidentally, was a born optimist. I had a long conversation with him. He said the day would come when the order to evacuate the settlements would be given, and the army would carry it out within two weeks.

He was, however, unusual. Much more frequent are encounters with CA officers who hound Palestinian shepherds or farmers off their lands. I've seen it countless times. There may be a bureaucratic twist added in for good measure. Once we were with shepherds grazing on their land in the wadi beneath Otniel. The soldiers, as always, tried to drive them off. We stood our ground. The senior CA officer was summoned. He pronounced as follows: the shepherds could of course graze their flocks on their land, but they had to coordinate first with the CA. This demand is routine, and routinely immoral; it requires an act of subservient recognition of the Occupation authority. Even the courts have sometimes recognized that it is illegal to require it. But on that particular morning, for various reasons it was important to let the grazing go forward without delay. So, restraining my rancor, I said to the officer: "Look, you're here and the shepherds are here; why not coordinate right now, if that's what you want?" "No," said the officer, "*they have to call us on the phone.*" "You mean," I said, "that because of this arbitrary technicality you are going to put a stop to their right to graze their sheep on their own land today?" He answered with one word: "Yes."

You can read many other examples in the pages below. Sometimes the officers exhibit a kind of bonhomie—they are convivial, not hostile, they shake hands and slap backs and speak politely to the Palestinians—but the outcome is, let me use the word again, entirely *wicked*. I have seen them drive away farmers who were clutching in hand the deeds to their lands, stamped and confirmed by the Israeli courts. Typical is the report from al-Tawamin (March 5, 2011), below.

I sometimes think that the bureaucratic impulse itself is wicked—a violent act of classifying in the interests of brute control. Many of those who work for the CA seem to me to be rigid, unimaginative persons who cling to the rules for dear life; and the rules have a life of their own. We all know such people from other domains, but the Occupation enhances exponentially their ability to do wrong and regularly exacerbates the cruelty of their decisions. We meet this reality face to face in the field. For all Palestinians living under the Occupation, daily life chugs along in a labyrinth of arbitrary regulations—permits to go here or there, permits to come home after visits abroad, permits to continue to reside in your own home and village, permits to live with your wedded spouse, permits to farm your land or graze your herds or draw water from your well. To call this labyrinth Kafkaesque would be to pay it an undeserved compliment: it is far beyond anything Kafka imagined. In addition, I believe that it was conceived and elaborated to the tortuous point of today's practice with deliberate, if perhaps uneven, intention.

And there is still worse to come. All evidence on the ground points to the existence of senior CA bureaucrats who are motivated by outright malice. I don't know these men—I assume they are male—for they inhabit a shadowy world of desks and air-conditioned offices and computers. But it is, I think, safe to infer their motivations from ongoing operations in the villages. Someone issues demolition orders on the surviving homes of Palestinian Susya—the whole of the village. Someone sends the bulldozers and the soldiers to knock down the dilapidated shacks at Umm al-Khair. Someone issues the order to destroy the entirely benevolent infrastructures of wind turbines and electric power that our activists have put in place in *khirbehs* throughout South Hebron. The CA will, of course, claim that the shacks and the turbines were built without permits, which is true—as I have said, Palestinians have almost no chance of getting a permit to build anywhere in South Hebron. Permits are issued, if at all, by a committee composed mostly of settlers that meets in the army camp at Beit El. The technicalities, indeed the entire abstract language of permits and approvals, are profoundly corrupt from start to finish. They embody malice of a high order, different in kind from the indeterminate wickedness of the courts or the police.

Recently a particularly trenchant example came to light, again with reference to Susya. The Palestinians from Susya, with mass demolition orders hanging over their heads, were told they could submit a development plan for the village which, if accepted by the authorities, would put a temporary end to the threat of expulsion. The relevant authority is a sub-committee of the Civil Administration; Susya submitted a very reasonable plan for its future, and in November 2013 the sub-committee duly rejected it. The interesting part was their reasoning:

"This plan offers no hope that the population can be advanced beyond the state of poverty and ignorance to which its representatives have condemned it. . . . The city, as the meeting place of diverse populations, serves as a source of cultural, economic, and educational enrichment. On the other side of the scale, the village dwellings are fragmented and scattered, founded upon tribal and clan identities which suffocate the citizen, the individual, and which offer no means for social development or opportunities for making a living, for cultural or educational experience. . . . The urban structure lets people meet one another, multiplies opportunities, enriches the horizons of each and every one in the family or tribe as in the wider society. Thus, in our view, the present plan is but another attempt to prevent this impoverished population from making progress. . . . It also prevents the Palestinian woman from liberating herself from the cycle of poverty and closes off opportunities for work and education. Similarly it keeps the Palestinian child away from the opportunities open to everyone else and condemns him to life in a small, degenerate village."

Perhaps nowhere in the world do we still hear such tones, which would have been well suited to French Algeria or a host of other colonial regimes. We can hear the white man's patronizing claim to know what's best for the "degenerate" dark man, even if it means uprooting him from his home and fields, stripping him of his livelihood and thus condemning him to rootless poverty, and, worst of all, destroying his entire culture. Sadly, this cynical document is all too typical of the Civil Administration; it is, moreover, driven by greed that has the temerity to mask itself in a rhetoric of progress. Here is wickedness that demands no further analysis, a form of violence far worse, and far more consequential, than outright physical attacks by settlers on Palestinian civilians. There are those who are capable of killing a man or a woman or a child, and there are those who take delight in killing a person's *right* to exist as an autonomous being—the latter case often preceding and justifying the former. We have come a long way from S. and his unconscious dilemmas.

Soldiers

More than anyone I have encountered, these are the people who most often experience themselves as helpless, lacking agency and choice. Possibly helplessness is a direct consequence of having to carry around lethal weapons. In any case, the fact that these weapons give you the power to kill in no way alleviates the awful sense that you have lost autonomy—that you have become, in your own right, not much more than a piece of disposable equipment. I remember it well. To demand personal choice under such circumstances is to stretch our faith in the human being beyond its common limits. Yet we do make this demand, and soldiers are held responsible for what they do, including—especially—acts that in Israel are categorized as falling under a "black flag"—a reference to a massacre by soldiers of innocent Palestinian farmers in Kafr Qasim in 1956. The soldiers followed the illegal orders they were given, and shot.

In the past, and perhaps, hopefully, still today, the Israeli army has told its new recruits that they are duty bound to resist illegal orders. What does this mean for the soldiers we encounter in South Hebron? I've never seen a single one resist orders that are incontrovertibly illegal under Israeli law—for example, the arbitrary imposition of a Closed Military Zone that means Palestinian farmers or shepherds are kept away from their lands. And there are far more radical examples. What about the soldiers who stand by passively as settlers beat Palestinian civilians, including schoolchildren, or Israeli activists—or who actively join in the violence, as happened at Umm al-Ara'is on November 23, 2013? And what about the whole corrupt regime of theft and dispossession? Or, to make things even more concrete, what about the deliberate harassment of Palestinians in their villages or, at times, at the countless roadblocks scattered through the territories? If you have any doubts about any of this, the volume of personal testimonies by soldiers who served in the territories, published by Breaking the Silence,[8] will, alas, put them to rest.

I don't want to belabor this point. There is too much to say, and it's usually far from clear when the need to resist might become pressing enough to elicit real thought, to say nothing of action. For now suffice it to say that the soldiers I meet in South Hebron are almost always ordinary people, no more wicked than anyone else, or than I am—indeed much less harmful than, say, the bureaucrats just mentioned. Some of them are astonishingly foolish in their ways of being, but foolishness is only sometimes wicked.

However, I have seen a few, very few, soldiers enacting cruelty with evident pleasure. Two officers, in particular, come to mind. There are many ways to drive a person off his or her land. It always hurts, of course. But young, rigid men in positions of authority may make it hurt even more. One of these officers not only pushed the shepherds, and us, off the lands he had marked off on his map of the CMZ but continued prodding all of us, step by awful step, deep into the desert while he mocked our protests. It went on for a long time, and we walked a long way. I think he liked doing it. The other one, on a different occasion, was no less pitiless. His spitefulness was accompanied by a sentence he kept repeating, when we protested: "I work for the battalion commander"—who, in this case, is a kind of all-powerful god. Such men, and others like them, will be good candidates for the International Court of Justice in the Hague.

How it happens that a person turns his innerness into an arid zone is a fascinating question. For soldiers, it may be a way, maybe the only way, to survive. We won't get anywhere by blaming them for it. In fact, blaming, in general, is too facile an escape. It is also a little too easy to speak about the evidently prevalent mechanism of dissociation, an inner blankness that allows you to commit violent crimes without feeling much of anything. Soldiers quite often tell us, even with a certain perverse pride, that they feel nothing when they carry out their orders. Once, when we heard a sentence like that, my friend Gabi said to the young soldier, "But that is when you are here, right? Not when you're at home with your friends and family." "No," said the soldier, "I don't feel anything there either."

Dissociation is, in a way, the least of it. Dissociation is much more than a habit; it is presumably motivated by internal forces, such as the unconscious or half-conscious struggle between benevolent and malevolent impulses, or by the active residues of severe trauma, or by the failure of hope. In South India, this numbing of feeling—either through involuntary entropy or through persistent inattention, which may also include an element of choice—is seen as the deepest human problem and the fundamental source of wickedness, and of suffering. After half a century of occupation, numbness of this order is, I think, endemic to the Israeli male. Somewhere, beneath all the rest, there exists terrible inner pain, compounded by fear and hatred, experienced as a kind of deadness. From within that pervasive deadness, many readily torment others. Once a person starts down this path, he or she normally keeps going; and someone will always be there to issue the relevant orders.

The Security Goon

Once I was sent off by Ezra Nawi to try to help some Palestinian who had been arrested out on the hills. We had no more information than that. We didn't even know where they'd taken him. For an hour or more my friend and I climbed up and down the rocks, hoping to find a trace. Another Palestinian appeared on a donkey and told us to follow him, but he then quickly disappeared: you perhaps have no idea how fast a donkey can run. Eventually we reached the main north-south highway and saw a clump of soldiers and other people, about half a kilometer away. We walked down to them. There were three Palestinian men, looking forlorn and frightened, and five or six policemen and soldiers, and a plain-clothes intelligence goon from one of the secret services, and a young, long-haired settler with a torn shirt. I asked them what had happened. The intelligence goon said at once, savoring each syllable: "A Jew has been attacked in South Hebron."

I can't say what really happened. Somewhere out on the hills there was an altercation between a Palestinian shepherd and some settlers. The settlers claimed that they'd been attacked. The Palestinians told a mirror-image story. Such things happen all the time. The point is the goon's obvious delight.

What was he thinking? It's not hard to imagine. Israeli Jews (like many Palestinians) love to feel victimized—it's a kind of base awareness, though not an innocent kind. It's perhaps linked both to the numbness I've just mentioned and to the hatred that numbness conceals—hence the common descent into wickedness. In this case, the soldiers of course carted off the Palestinian, whom they'd accused, to some police station or military camp. We couldn't prevent it. His hope of finding justice, were they to bring him to court, was nil. I don't know how the case developed. I never even knew his name.

But that sentence went on echoing in my memory. "A Jew has been attacked in South Hebron." The goon didn't know he was gloating. He may well have felt that he was reconnected to a very ancient chain of attacks on members of his tribe. And anyway he chose to be a goon, so he was perhaps disposed from the start to see things in that light. I wouldn't want to know what other sorts of things this man may have done or witnessed in the course of his years of service. What I do know is that I felt his words to be pregnant with self-righteous violence. I'm sure it never even occurred to him that the settler—whether or not he was attacked—had no business being in South Hebron in the first place. Hearing what he said, with its assumption that any Jewish person would accept it and identify with it as he did, I felt a visceral disgust. Wickedness easily masks itself as other things—solidarity, for example, or even sincere solicitude for the members of your own tribe at the expense of all others. On the other hand, wickedness masquerading as kindness is always transparent, unlike the wickedness that is a form of dullness or torpor.

Willful Passivity

I began with the bullies and I am ending with the torpid; along the way, many of the wicked have been left out of this account. There's no need to list them here; all of us have a part in the continuing horror of the Occupation. But certain themes keep recurring as I reflect and as I write. Let me try to formulate them one last time.

I think wickedness as we commonly encounter it, or as we enact it in ourselves, is a very subtle business, a matter of shifting, ephemeral sub-tectonic slips. It is a whole-person act, not a dichotomous black-and-white division in the self but a flesh-and-blood sort of thing, rooted not in moral clarity—itself a rare thing—but in moral ambiguity, the true ground of almost all human action. We act not in spite of but because of ambiguity. Within a field that is open to all sorts of readings, that is complex beyond even what we can formulate in language, we make our choices and we speak our words, true or false words as the case may be.

If I have argued that wickedness needs to be seen as belonging to the whole person, it is not in the sense that the person is wholly wicked—such cases are rare—but in the sense that the whole person decides, within the margin of her freedom, whether to do the wicked thing or not. When I say decision, I am not referring to a reflective and conscious choice but to the kind of choice that is made through some unruly and often conflicted configuration of inner circumstances, as in most of our consequential decisions. Such choices, in my view, tend to be slight movements within the self, if self there be. Very often they could go otherwise. In fact, I would want to argue for an even more radical theory of unreflective freedom to choose. Without such a postulate, it is impossible to speak meaningfully about Ezra's judge, Ms. Ziskind, or about S., my police-officer friend. Nor could we speak, without this notion of an indeterminate and mostly ambiguous ground for action, about the possibility, however remote, for remorse, atonement, and forgiveness.

A subtle imbalance may exist at any moment, for each of us. Usually, faced with the dim awareness of the choice, or without any such awareness, we slip into the well-oiled groove of habit and collective passivity. Subtlety and slippage belong together. However, we do not have to slip. In some sense, we *will* our slippage. Only the person as a whole can slip. Clear intention may not come into play. But if we reflect upon our ways of being and thinking, especially in situations of severe conflict like in Palestine and Israel, we may recognize in ourselves a will not to know, or not to know that we know, and, above all, not to act. Knowledge comes with a price. Willfulness of this sort, even if it is unconscious, lies at the heart of complicity with what is wicked and may be the single most powerful factor in giving wickedness room to do its worst.

One possible moral aim, in conditions such as those I've described, would be a micro-incremental enhancement of the inner freedom to choose without slippage. I'm not very hopeful about the chances of any one among us achieving this, including me. However, I have seen the Indian non-dual episteme—the assertion that knowledge of our deeper selves exists inside us as perhaps our most hidden but most momentous form of knowing—enacted, sometimes dramatically, before my eyes. In such cases, timing matters. Someone might whisper a word meant for someone else that, overheard, changes your life. Sometimes it happens even without the whisper.

An important consequence we can derive from such a view is that wickedness is not and cannot be banal. In fact, nothing could be less banal than evil, coming as it does from those subtle surfaces within us where choice lurks, unknown to us. Of course, to the victim of wickedness, wickedness is never banal; and possibly one might say the same thing about the passive witness (who tends to play a critical role). Even Hannah Arendt did not really mean that evil itself was banal; her claim was that the evildoer, such as Eichmann, was so impoverished in his own personhood that he acted in a horrifically superficial way, without being able to think. For Arendt, like for Socrates, good thinking—nontrivial, rational thought—could and should preclude acting wickedly. I think, however, that even this notion of impoverished and unthinking personhood is mostly wrong. Wickedness is a whole-person move, whether active or passive, aware or unaware. (We now know that Arendt was dead wrong about Eichmann.) It could also be the case that what we are talking about implies the radical coincidence of surface and depth, which is not so much an ethical notion as a cosmological one.

To be fair, I want to say that, in some auspicious cases, there is a happy coincidence of choice and good luck. It doesn't hurt to be lucky about such things as our own wickedness.

Thus I end with a surprising conclusion, unforeseen when I started reflecting about these things, about the subtle zone of choice, usually exercised in wicked ways. Lest you think me overly sanguine about what human beings are and what they do, I take refuge in William Butler Yeats's lines from the "Prayer for My Daughter." What Yeats wrote is that "hearts are not had as a gift but hearts are earned/ by those who are not entirely beautiful." By "beautiful" he meant, I think, "good"— these categories merge in Yeats, indeed in many great poets. So "hearts are not had as a gift but hearts are earned/ by those who are not entirely good." This is my paraphrase, which I know is true to my own life.

Acts of subtle wickedness, of inner hardening and encrustation, of cowardly passivity in the face of evident cruelty—they are the stuff of our lives, day after day, and, sadly, they have a way of cumulating in the social and political worlds we inhabit to the point where pure, systemic wickedness takes over and choice narrows to a tiny margin. It can happen anywhere; there is never any dearth of sadists who have power, who feed off these micro-decisions we make, individually and together, by the million. As Joachim Prinz, who had first-hand experience of Germany in the 1930s, said during the March on Washington in 1963:

"I was the rabbi of the Jewish community in Berlin under the Hitler regime. I learned many things. The most important thing that I learned in my life is that bigotry and hatred are not the most urgent problem. The most urgent, the most disgraceful, the most shameful, and the most tragic problem is silence."

In extreme situations, such as what we have today in Israel-Palestine, much depends—maybe everything depends—on the actions of ordinary, decent people who confront the subtleties I've been speaking about. Not on what such people think, but on what they choose to do.

4

FREEDOM

1.

Take it as an axiom that no Israeli will ever be free until Palestine is free. Almost without exception, our Palestinian friends in the South Hebron hills have never known even a single hour of freedom, at least not in the last fifty years. They may be free, in an important sense, in their hearts and minds, but they are confronted with an external reality of state terror that hurts them, continually hems them into tiny spaces in which they can somehow, barely, live their lives, and that is, in general, getting heavier and harder to bear week by week. There is a bitter contrast between the wide-open vistas of the desert and the utter absence of freedom to move, even to breathe, that lies at the base of their experience. There is constant danger as well. For this reason, it is they who know what freedom really means. They sometimes speak of it, usually a little tentatively or obliquely, as if not wishing to compromise a sacred dimension of living that is denied them. On the other hand, if one spends time with them in their homes and fields and grazing grounds, one may well discover a certain grace under conditions of external harshness and gratuitous cruelty. It requires no little courage to live in the desert with little water and without freedom, and this natural courage is perhaps their most salient trait, evident in the way they move through space and time.

But what might freedom mean to us, Israeli activists, who may even take it, unthinkingly, as our birthright, but who have come down to South Hebron to take part in this struggle? To be honest, our relations with freedom, whatever it is, are usually obscure, though acting in a good cause may clarify them in unexpected ways. In the following pages, I will be speaking mostly of my own experiences and those of my colleagues, which may well resonate strongly with those of many Palestinian friends I have known; but I will not try to speak for them. It is for them to say.

I found freedom, of a certain kind, in the hills of South Hebron. It was a surprise. The discovery of one's own profound freedom always comes as a surprise. Human beings, in general will do everything they can to deny themselves this knowledge. Why they should do so is one of the mysteries. In my case, not looking for it, I stumbled on my freedom, in the inevitably limited forms it can take. I was free long before I knew I was free.

How can that be possible? But is this not our usual state, the baseline of human awareness? I have this to do, and that. I have to eat several times a day. I feel desire that demands, and never accepts, satisfaction. Some day I will die, unwillingly. Why, then speak of freedom?

Like happiness, freedom eludes the person who pursues it deliberately. There is something oblique about it, as with so much of our experience, especially our experience of things that are beyond doubt. To come to know this business of freedom, I have to act. Freedom of the kind that is relevant here is not a passive state, not, at base, a surrender. It is innately active, even if the process begins only in the mind. I think of it as an active movement of the mind in its hunger for such things as self-knowledge or for anything that suggests or enhances its own aliveness. Since we are perpetually compromising our own aliveness, we need continuously to reinvent the conditions of our freedom. Every time we fail to do this—as happens to all of us many times each day, perhaps each hour—we once again bind ourselves to a rock like the one Sisyphus keeps rolling uphill.

No one needs yet another philosophical essay on freedom; it's one of those subjects with many words piled up around it, shutting out the light. We might do well, first, to free ourselves from some of the words. Freedom, if it exists, may inhabit a zone somewhere in the midst of the pile; perhaps one could burrow one's way into it. I propose to follow a different course.

I am standing on some barren hill or field, and the officer tells me to leave, threatening me with punishments of variable severity if I stay. I say no. It happens all the time. That "no" at once enlarges and defines my freedom. I had to learn how to say it, the inner cadence and rhythm of a true no. But it's no good speaking in generalities. Here is one short, low-key example.

2.
April 5, 2008, Umm Zeituna

Ahmad is nonchalant, almost serene, smoking the cigarettes he's been gifted by Amiel; every once in a while, he moves, with astonishing grace, to turn a sheep back from the slope, to shape and mold the grazing, bleating herd. He seems subtly alert to the physical presence of each of his animals, some hundred in all; he holds them in his mind even as he sings a few snatches of song, teases us for our broken Arabic, tries to fill in the contours of some mental picture of our urban world, so remote from his. He accepts us as if we were simply another piece of this jagged landscape of thorn and stone and grass, with the occasional eagle overhead, and the dark perimeter of his settler enemies a mere two hundred yards away, riding the hill. This is his wadi, his father's grazing ground, the land of his father's father and so on back to the beginning of time, and without us he would not be here today.

I soak in the sun. I am in mourning. On Sunday Gerald died, a friend of infinite closeness; he was sixty-three. Cancer ate through his body with lightning speed—a mere six weeks ago he was vigorous and apparently well. A man of total integrity, a fighter, a Jew of the old school, a religious humanist, dedicated to doing what was just, and to peace. I cannot understand why I am drinking in this sunlight and tasting the dry wind from the desert and the smells of cigarette smoke and sheep dung and wildflowers, and he can no longer feel. I puzzle at this with my mind, sadness welling up through my veins. I turn back to Ahmad with a question. And then they are upon us.

We expected it, after all. A group of settlers from Maon is racing downhill toward us, crying out their throaty battle cries—not words but grunts and hisses and clicks and, from time to time, a menacing scream. There are three in the lead: one in sandals, long white shirt, long blond hair, wild eyes, the mandatory fringes of his Talit dancing as he runs; a second with face masked by a black cloth, leaving only a slit for the eyes; a third more heavyset and ungainly. Behind them, still high on the hill, are more. All right, I say to myself, ready to act: Gerald, this one is for you.

We fan out over the hilltop as the Palestinians cluster with the herd in the wadi below us. We try, at first successfully, to block the settlers' access. They weave around us among the stones, cursing now and crying: "*Ufu mipo*, Get the hell out of here." We cut them off, again and again, but still they are starting to close in on our friends. Somewhere my mind registers the fact that, for once, they are not carrying guns. On the other hand, a handful of soldiers are also fast approaching from the direction of Maon—a sergeant and several privates. The settlers reach the bed of the wadi and, circling past the shepherds, begin driving the sheep before them, out and away.

We invoke the "law," for what it's worth: these shepherds have the right to graze in this wadi, there's a document signed by the *matak,* the senior officer in this area. . . . But the sergeant is scornful of such niceties. "Don't talk to me," he says, "and don't tell me what to do." To his privates, he remarks with derision: "Look at them, it's like kids in elementary school." To us, after a moment's reflection, walking fast, he says: "I don't incline to either side here. Get out." And who are we to tell him that his very presence, guns and all, is what allows these settlers to go on living in Maon and Susya and Carmel—that it is he, by sustaining them here, who allows them to prey upon the shepherds, to beat them and humiliate them and take away their land?

Amiel sends me to stand on the far side of the herd, to keep them from running away as the settlers want them to. I'm not so good at masterminding sheep. In fact, these sheep seem to me imbued with a Zen-like emptiness; they ebb and flow, responding rapidly to the rough shouts of the settlers, who are poking and pushing them toward the end of the wadi, and then, in sudden reversal, to the shepherds' commands to turn back. Every few seconds a fuzzy wave of sheep and goats washes across the wadi floor in some new direction, uphill and down, northward or southward, lapping at the gray boulders, trickling past the whole surreal congregation of helmeted soldiers and settlers in their Sabbath white and the impassive shepherds and our now furious activists. In the midst of these ovine eddies, there is a steady stream of invective flowing toward us: "You filthy Nazis," the settlers scream, and so on, the usual unimaginative pastiche. The blond one, his face contorted, grotesque in hate, suddenly rushes down the slope and smashes into Amiel. "Did you see that?" I say to the sergeant. "Arrest him! Look who's being violent here." "Don't tell me how to do my job," says the sergeant, bored, detached. "I told you not to talk to me."

Minutes pass. One of the settlers lashes out at Efrat; Amiel, ever chivalrous, rushes in to defend her. "We have the right to hit them, that's what the Torah says, doesn't it?" one settler shouts to his friend, obviously an authority on Biblical hermeneutics. Still busy containing the sheep, I manage somehow to reflect on what I'm feeling. I wonder, for example, if there is hatred in my heart. I scan my innerness as best I can: no trace of hate this time. No fear either. Perhaps, by now, after so many of these clashes, I'm inured. But I'm definitely a person who *can* hate, that I know. I repeat the scan. There is fierce anger, no doubt about that. Also, I am ashamed to report, something verging on contempt. I see their brittle certainty, hear the crude insults they are shouting, note the frightened, impoverished manhood of the bully. OK, so I feel contempt. I wish I could work myself up to something better.

By now the settlers have been joined by their security officer, carrying an M-16. Definitely not a friendly presence. He ardently hopes, so he tells us, that our Palestinian friends will stab us in the back when we're asleep. He's pretty sure that they do this regularly. Meanwhile Efrat, delicate, focused, and wonderfully self-possessed, has had enough, and she says to him in crisp rapid fire, each syllable ringing out distinctly in the desert air: "Maybe you're a killer, too. We don't know. What we know for sure is that you're a thief." "A thief?" he replies, rising to the bait, "at least I care about the Jews, and I'm prepared to give my life for my country." "I hope you won't have to do that," I say to him, breaking my own rule: don't engage in banter with the enemy. He turns to me. "And you," he says, livid with hatred, "would you give your life for this country?" "Most definitely not," I answer. I really don't like the idea. In fact, standing there amid the sheep, I find it hard to think of a worthy enough cause. Is there such a thing? Flags, postage stamps, and Independence Day parades are clearly out. My children, grandchildren, wife, friends, my students—yes. No question. But for a state? Maybe, I think to myself, a little whimsically, I'd risk it for the sake of some amorphous notion of integrity. In order to do the decent thing. In order to feel again this strange, unexpected, utterly intoxicating feeling of being free, truly and deeply and shockingly free, that I'm becoming aware of at this moment as the sun burns through my skin. It has something to do with standing my ground in the face of violence and with saying "no," or "Do what you like, but I won't go along with this, nor will I get sucked into the vortex of the lie." It feels good, no doubt about that, but this is not the goodness of pleasure, at least not as we usually use that word. It feels good because it is right.

The soldiers stand more or less between the warring camps; our settler foes are but a pace away. It is Shabbat, almost noon. Amiel deliberately, with excruciating precision, lights a cigarette—almost as serious a crime, in the settlers' eyes, as befriending a Palestinian; a violation of God's commandment for this day of rest. (What rest?) They watch him in disgust. Though I don't much like smoking and usually feel unwell afterward, I briefly consider whether, under present circumstances, to light my own cigarette might be the Jewish thing to do, an affirmation that God exists.

3.

That's the no that matters most. I might not have dragged God into it if a few days before this incident one of the settler Rabbis had not published a legal opinion setting out a calculus of human value: one Jew, said the Rabbi, is worth a thousand Palestinian lives.

"No," the music of defiance, is a word that, in critical situations, creates the alive human person. I stand in the middle ground between the attackers and their victims, I am doing my best to protect the latter and also to take care of my friends and colleagues, and no matter what happens to me, by standing there I am saying "no." This word has the most remarkable plenum of being that flows inside it. It must be the most capacious and elastic word in the language, any language. It can unravel in a second the whole tissue of lies that we live with hour by hour, especially those that envelop us on all sides from without, the specious inanities of the government and the self-righteous mendacity of the nationalists. "No" belongs to the zone of risk. It's like alchemy: you take the risk, opening yourself to it out of the most diverse and paltry motives, you embody the protest, and the next thing you know is that you are a little freer. But there is a necessary condition: the freedom that is ours to win comes from the attempt, successful or not, to enhance the freedom of another being, whereas even the slightest complicity in denying another's freedom condemns the denier to servitude.

There is a yes hidden inside this no, an affirmation that life is worth living, especially if one refuses to go along with the herd, to be complicit in the wickedness of the herd, to submit to what the herd demands. I say no: do what you want to me, punish me, attack me, but I am not going to budge from this hilltop you have stolen. I will stand here and bear witness against you, if need be until the end of time. My whole body cries no to your crime. This no is my no, but not mine alone; the universe resonates to the sound of a refusal to do wrong.[9]

Some people are driven, from within, to saying no. Among recent examples, we have the statements of Sahar Vardi and Tair Kaminer, both young women who refused to serve in the army of occupation. Such a refusal is always a highly personal choice, and no one should be in the position of asking others to make it. But the consequential *no* echoes loudly through their words. Here is what Sahar wrote as she went with open eyes into a military prison for refusing to be inducted in the army. The text requires no further comment.

> I first set eyes on the Occupation as a twelve-year-old girl. It was in a small Palestinian village southwest of Jerusalem inhabited by some twenty-five families, most of whom were well educated, building contractors, Palestinian authority employees, and so on. They did not seem any different to me than most people I saw walking down the streets. The only visible difference was that they had green ID cards.
>
> As a twelve-year-old who came to the village to replace the one-inch water pipe with a two-inch pipe, I did not understand the full meaning of the different color of the ID, but I did understand the simple meaning: separation. The fact that the road to the village from Jerusalem was blocked by the IDF, the fact that a fence separated the village from its neighboring village, along with the different IDs—all

of these came to separate me from "them" and to prove beyond a doubt that we are not equal.

I was brought up at school, and at home as well, on the so-called obvious core values such as justice, freedom, human rights, and equality; but now I found out, before I even began junior high, that the state in which I live does not care for these values, and not only does it not care for them, it violates them and suppresses millions of people so that I could enjoy the "freedom" they taught me everyone deserves.

I have visited the occupied territories countless times, and as much as I have tried to convince myself that the soldier in the checkpoint is not to be blamed for the repressive policy of Israel, I cannot strip that soldier of responsibility for his own actions. I am speaking not only of the political implications of guarding a settlement, or of the legal implications of the murders we perform in the occupied territories. I speak of the human responsibility each of us has not to harm our fellow man.

The clause in the Geneva Convention that speaks of freedom of thought, conscience, and religion grants every person the right to act or refuse to act according to his or her conscience; but in my opinion it is not a matter of right, but of obligation. It is our obligation as human beings not to hurt others, to protect their rights and to treat others as we would wish to be treated ourselves. If this is our obligation, is it not our obligation to refuse to take part in any action that includes harming others, even one that we are obliged to perform by law? Do we not have the moral, human, and even legal obligation to refuse to deprive people of their freedom of movement, of housing, and above all—of the right to live?

For all of these reasons, I cannot stand in a checkpoint and separate one race from another, one ID from another, and I cannot bomb cities filled with men women and children even if in war, and I cannot punish millions of innocents for the crimes of few. This is not only because I refuse to be a pawn of politicians, but because I refuse to cause suffering. I refuse to act violently whether under orders or not.

The cycle of bloodshed in which I live, the cycle made up of bombings and suicide attacks and shootings, with more and more victims on both sides, is perpetuated by the choice of both sides to react violently. I refuse to be a part of that choice.

4.

Clearly, we are not speaking about just any sort of defiance. Stated minimally, in the light of Sahar's words: Under no circumstances will I be a party to the torture of another human being. Nor will I enslave others or steal what is theirs. To the best of my ability, I will reject and defy any system built upon such forms of torture. Whatever else drives me to go down to South Hebron, again and again, this principle must also be in play. It conditions the peculiar form my freedom takes in the field.

So there is this thought, conscious and clear, that comes with straightforward criteria to apply to its enactment. However, I want to reach down to another level of our existence, unfortunately with little but my own experience to rely on. People committed to strong notions of conscious rationality in the Western template often claim that human reason enables and shapes our freedom. I disagree. I know that I am free before I think about it. I know it because I am alive.

Perhaps it has something to do with the particular personhood that applies to me in the culture I inhabit. Whole civilizations deny this—depersonalization, or radical de-individuation, may be the path to a release that is defined as freedom. Even in the West, there is never any lack of voices calling for the suppression of ego and self-driven need. I am suspicious of such voices. Though I neither selected my own name, nor chose the language that came first or the number of nerve cells I possess or the color of my eyes, I have no doubt that much of the time I am someone, not anyone, and that at times, at least, I can choose how to act.

Choice is not always a faultless indication of inner freedom. On the other hand, certain choices may suggest that there is some room to maneuver, as I argued in discussing wickedness. That small space, the gap between all that conditions me and the theoretical unpredictability of my thoughts and actions, intrigues me. South Hebron has offered ample opportunity to explore it.

In some sense, it is that small space that indexes my aliveness. Hannah Arendt writes of the freedom that comes with the birth of a human being, with "natality" itself; but this is a freedom that waits to be actualized in word and deed.[10] What sort of word? "No," for example, under the ethical conditions I have outlined. Note that enacting one's freedom in this way— growing into it, perhaps—is quite different from "the daring of adventure which gladly risks life for the sake of being thoroughly and intensely alive."[11] For Hannah Arendt, that daring is of a lesser order than the courage needed to reveal oneself for who one is—possibly the political act par excellence. It is that kind of act, requiring speech, that triggers the sense of a deeper aliveness, itself an expression of human freedom. This intricate linkage between an existential freedom and the thrill of aliveness, and between these two and moral action, was something

I had to learn from experience. A moral act is immeasurably more powerful than the "daring of adventure," and far more likely to render the actor free.

5.

Let's go back to that moment when the happiness of freedom began in the rocky wadi, amid the sheep and goats and soldiers and settlers. With some hesitation, I can try to analyze it further. Maybe it's entirely idiosyncratic. Maybe it masks a deeper and more painful sense of un-freedom—of being at the mercy of these soldiers and settlers and of the state itself, of being trapped by wickedness. Un-freedom does, I think, usually and dependably inhabit the free space that turns up to surprise me.

How has this moment unfolded? I've already spoken about the risk, and about the moral substrate. But the stronger and more interesting part has to do with the sense that something inside has shifted with no effort on my part. It's as if the habitual noise of my mind, the endless hubbub of *me*, had been hushed, at least for that moment. Risk allows this to happen. I think this is the principle that molds the agonistic wherever we find it. Fate, an aspect of freedom, is regularly generated from within the zone of risk.

It can feel like an intoxicant, this giddy free-ness. I've learned not to overdo it. In fact, even as that strange happiness wells up inside me, I become aware of a sober riptide. Is there such a thing as an intoxicating sobriety? There's so much to be said for being sober—for the wholeness and clarity that, with luck, can characterize and define sobriety. Thus along with the rush of joy, I have the sense of standing on solid ground in a world that has lost none of its baffling opacity.

All this happens quickly. Fear may be present (it's a good thing, fear, an evolutionary good); but the only courage that is required to enable freedom to appear is the courage not to bring the clutter back to the front of your mind. One really has to leave the space open. An open space threatens us so profoundly that we immediately rush in, with mad impetuousness, to fill it with whatever comes to hand. So in the middle of the delicious feeling in my body, beginning somewhere in my toes and spreading unevenly but very powerfully upward into my fingertips, my neck, my spine, my mouth, and the physical inside of my head, not in that order, in the middle of its sudden and fleeting rampage through me, I start to think: "Look at that, I am feeling free again." Or, rationalizing: "At least I'm doing the right thing, or the closest I can get to it." Or: "How many times do I have to go through this?" Or: "This is ridiculous." Or: "Why am I doing this anyway?" Or: "The settlers are X (vicious, primitive, childish, etc.), and as for the soldiers. . . ." Or: "I can't stand this (feeling so free) another minute." Or: "This will be worth reporting on and who knows, I might even write an essay on freedom." Those kinds of thoughts turn up, though please remember that quite a lot is happening outside and there's sometimes danger and I also have to act and sometimes to speak.

Sometimes at such moments I feel like laughing, as if a tension within me sought release by emptying itself out into the world. Moreover, I always feel this freedom as something that is indubitable and also singularly mine. I think each of the others may have his or her own variety of it, but still there remains a personal quality to this brief flaring up of feeling. I wouldn't want to generalize or make it into some sort of absolute. Perhaps because it's so private, perhaps because communicating about it directly may damage it, perhaps out of fear or shyness or even shame, perhaps because along with the rush of happiness there is also a countervailing sense of constriction and imminent sorrow, I don't feel like asking my friends if they know what I'm talking about.

There's something more, another unexpected discovery. As the horizon shifts, I can see my kinship with the settler who is screaming at me at this very moment. Indeed, if I can't see it, I am as constricted as he is. Of course, I may also feel rage and I will think, consciously, that I am right and he is wrong. There is, however, little freedom in being right. Possibly, I have encompassed his hatred, his narrowness, his mistake, his human failure, which is not far removed from my own consistent failures. I am not speaking metaphorically. It helps that in my own eyes I am "right" in a general way vis-à-vis the political reality and the ethical frame and other such things, but it is not this intellectual conviction that explains or determines the strange expansion of my horizon and the rush of understanding—let us call it understanding, for want of a better term. It is connected to a passing sense that life is suddenly more real and more complete than I had imagined it before this moment, and that even a tiny act of resistance on my part has helped to bring my world alive.

But deep inside this complex set of perceptions is the awareness that, whatever is going on in me, our Palestinian shepherd and his friends can't share much of it. We're here for their sake, and they are, as always, stuck in helplessness. The system in its routine violence has struck again, and they can at best hope only to survive this moment without too much damage, without arrest or physical attack. It is possible, I think, that in some deep part of themselves they retain inviolability, perhaps akin to a tenuous sense of freedom, even under conditions of external violation. And perhaps the malevolent denial of freedom leads eventually, inexorably, to the moment when freedom will be reclaimed, for freedom is perhaps what human beings need and long for above all. In any case, the solidarity I feel with them, and the anguish that arises at this moment, are intrinsic to the sense of some shift inside me.

By now my description has lasted much longer than the quiver itself. It tends to be quite fleeting. But it's not just a flash: there's an oddly stable quality about it—familiar, too, as if it were something I knew quite well without being able to access it regularly. Sober, real, unmistakable, consequential, put-together—words like that might characterize this state. And it's quite wrong to romanticize it (or, for that matter, deliberately to seek it); indeed, it's a sensation that is almost the opposite of our common slippage from one romantic illusion to another.

And when it's over, you don't feel empty or let down or confused or awkward, as one might after sexual loving, for example. This fact alone, an empirical observation under laboratory conditions in the South Hebron hills, may be the most telling evidence I have that freedom is—as so many have claimed—some fundamental part of our nature. I protest, therefore I am. I act, doing what I think is right, therefore I am. I am at risk, for a good reason, for some minimally acceptable reason, therefore I am. Conversely, I am, therefore I am free. Better still, I am me, therefore I am free.

At the height of it, I realize that it is this feeling, this particular form of understanding, that I have been seeking all along. I might even be a little grateful to the settlers and the soldiers for making it happen, furious as I may be as it happens. If that sounds mad, it's because one doesn't often get to know the sober madness at the outer edge of saying no. This rush of freedom flows counter to what we might expect. It is ours but not ours alone; it connects us to the other, especially the other whose freedom is compromised or threatened but who is suddenly, and deeply, part of us, as we are part of him or her. Freedom of this sort is not merely subjective; it is always intersubjective, intrinsically so. What is more, such freedom always strikes before one is prepared for it; and one knows it not at the first moment, but slightly later.

6.

Once I did ask my friend Maria Kharash how it feels to get arrested. She's by far the most outspoken, even blunt, of all the activists I've known, and I think for that very reason she belongs here, in this chapter.

It's not so easy to introduce Maria. I can tell you she's a musician. She has a way of cutting through heavy words. Once, after a typical day at Umm al-Ara'is, when we'd been driven away, as usual, by the soldiers, with some brutality, I said to her: "Sometimes I have this dream that all the nitpicking foolishness, the futile arguments over the Closed Military Zone, the idiotic arrests, all the threats and petty cruelty, and the not-so-petty kind, too, and the lies, and the greed, all of this will be washed by some huge wave into the sea." Maria said, "It will happen when this desert becomes a sea."

I asked her to tell me how she got into the South Hebron business. She said:

"Tamar brought me to Ta'ayush. I was sharing a flat with her in Bak'a. I was not active in the peace movement, none of that really interested me. I didn't serve in the army, I didn't read newspapers, I couldn't care less who the prime minister was. I worked in a bookstore. I lived for a year and a half in Portugal.

Worked at this and that, here and there. I thought I was here in order to study flute.

I was nine and a half years old when my parents took us here from St. Petersburg. They're both doctors. I got here for fifth grade in Haifa. I was in the Arts High School. I knew some Arabs. I volunteered in Magen David Adom, I would meet them there and elsewhere. It's a little different if you're an immigrant. Once I was talking with a friend about how we should live, say like hippies, as if it was a strange option, but it isn't; there are plenty of Bedouins here and other people who live outside society.

Tamar used to go to South Hebron. One Friday I said, "Maybe I'll come with you." But we hadn't registered. We came on Saturday morning and there was no room, so we went home. A year, maybe two, passed. Then one day in the winter, when Tamar was going, I came too. That first time there was a big deal at al-Tawamin and we got arrested, Tamar, me, Danny, and Nissim. The soldiers announced a Closed Military Zone, Amiel decided we would stay. At first Tamar and I moved back a little to avoid arrest and then we decided we'd stay too and see what happens. So we were arrested, and they released us that same evening. I said to myself: "This was nice" (*haya neh-mad*). So I came again.

I don't like demonstrations. It seems more right to do things like this [in South Hebron]. Doing things from inside. Maybe it has more effect than something external like going to a demonstration.

I like being outside. And I like the south. This, Ta'ayush, feels more real to me. You come and you act. And I like the people, the activists. There's a nice atmosphere. Nobody is sitting on top of you (*af ehad lo yoshev lecha al ha-vrid*) or telling you what to do. That suits me. It gives you your own space, and you make your choice."

ME: Do you feel anything of the pain of the Palestinians, their situation?

MARIA: I don't look at things like that. It's the life of a human being. I don't judge it. I don't feel pity.

ME: OK, but just two days ago you were driven off the land at Umm al-Ara'is together with Sa'id and the 'Awad clan. How does it feel?

MARIA: You get used to it.

"Sometimes I'm angry at the settlers or the soldiers. They irritate me, the lousy settlers and the lousy soldiers. I also don't feel guilty. Of course, it would be great if this whole situation didn't exist—if, for example, the Palestinians could decide they'd go to the beach on a Saturday. Anyway, I feel more despair at having to write my papers for the Music Academy than I do at Umm al-Ara'is.

ME: Getting arrested is sometimes sort of satisfying, isn't it?

MARIA: Yes, sometimes, but usually it doesn't feel so good. Sometimes you know it's for nothing. Sometimes there's no choice, and it happens very fast. Sometimes you get fed up and say, Yallah, let them arrest me already. Sometimes you think it's for the best. It can be a kind of experience, an adventure.

And there's getting beaten up. Omri and me are "Victims of Mizpeh Ya'ir." It was right at the beginning, when I started to come to Ta'ayush. They [the settlers] broke all the cameras and beat us up. We were arrested together with the Palestinians.

I don't think of myself as an idealistic person. I feel like what we do suits me, and it's right and just, and I'm at peace with it. I love the kids at Umm al-Ara'is.

My father says to me, "Why are you getting involved in something that's not connected to you?" He's right in a way.

But I said to him, "When my sister went into the army, why didn't you ask her that same question?" Serving in the army is also taking sides.

Once I was talking to a soldier at Umm al-Ara'is. I asked him what he was doing. He said, "I do what they tell me to do." "WHAT?" I said to him. He said, "I do what the flag tells me to do." "Hey man," I said to him, "you're talking with flags. You should be hospitalized."

7.

You're probably relieved. Maria can do that. Maybe freedom comes along with a strong dose of self-deprecating irony. Maybe it generates an inner distance from the feelings that well up. Maybe it makes one a little less eager to make judgments. It undoubtedly shuns anything that smacks of the sentimental and the moralistic.

We could stop here, with Maria, except for the fact that a problem still requires attention. I've described a kind of freedom that seems heavily subjective, though I have also claimed that it is naturally intersubjective, strongly infused with the world of feeling of others beside me, friends or foes. But is my experience of freedom any different from, let us say, the feeling of the settlers who attack us and scream obscenities at us, or from what the soldier feels, at moments, on the battlefield (whether he believes in the alleged purpose of the war or not)? What about the terrorist who throws off all constraints and delights in sheer destruction? Maybe any act of defiance, even the immature defiance-for-defiance's sake of the adolescent, will serve to generate some form of happiness.

No. There is a difference. The peculiar texture I identify

with freedom is not compatible with the violence of your run-of-the-mill soldier or with simple thuggery, the marauding settlers' mode. No doubt the settlers and the soldier sometimes have the same heady feel of acting—rationalized in all sorts of ways—but they would never recognize the freedom I'm talking about. For one thing, there's a huge amount of clutter in the way. I was once in a war, and I know something of what it's like. There's not the tiniest tinge of freedom. As for the settlers, full-blooded hatred precludes my kind of freedom. I have seen hatred in operation, I know it when I encounter it. It is as remote from a sense of freedom as anything could be. Full-fledged hatred distorts the features of the face, does something strange to the eyes, and feeds into a kind of awkward physical clutching, crippling the person invaded, or possessed, by this force. It looks demonic, like a stifled stasis. This is the case even if hatred is classed in the person's own mind as love—as sometimes happens—and even if his hatred *is*, in fact, a crooked transmutation of love.

Freedom is of a different order from any of these possible rivals. It is at once a necessary feature of our aliveness and, in becoming known to us, entirely contingent on circumstance. In case disciples of Kant are reading these lines, I should declare that I don't want anything like Kant's "absolute" or "transcendental" freedom—as if such a thing could be. I want the precarious freedom of a man who will die. The fact that I will die is one of the conditions of my freedom. Contingency is the key to recognizing it for what it is.[12]

Kant, as is well known, distinguished a somewhat limited and derivative "psychological freedom" from "transcendental freedom," without which "no moral law and no accountability to it are possible."[13] But where would I put a transcendental freedom in the hills of South Hebron? Could it survive outside amid the rocks and thorns? Could it heal the suffering of our friends, or the pain we feel with *their* pain? I say again: Give me contingent, embodied, transient, compromised freedom and its consequences. Give me a non-romantic freedom that may not even be able to distinguish between appearances and things-in-themselves, as Kant thought we needed to do in order to make any moral choice. In my own life, most of my moral choices, such as they were, emerged out of an ambiguous and murky jumble of appearances and realities. Is there any other ground for action?

My kind of contingent freedom cannot emerge from conditions of perverse moral perception or, a fortiori, from a benumbed failure to imagine some portion of the other's pain. In fact, my kind of freedom may well be, before all else, an imaginative act—before it takes the form of choice. If I cause gratuitous pain to another, even if I attempt to subsume that pain under some notion of its necessity for my own survival, freedom will flee from me even further and faster than it usually does. It's certainly possible to feel something like *release* or *disinhibition* or, for that matter, sadistic delight in causing pain to another, all this under what I have called perverse moral conditions. Such feelings have nothing in common with freedom.

8.

As I write, images of Palestinian friends, peace activists, keep popping into my mind. Many of them, like Ali Abu Awad, like Osama Elawat, like Abdallah Abu Rahmah, spent years in Israeli prisons. They know more about freedom than I do. They know about insufferably long deprivation, about being subject to arbitrary humiliation on an hour-to-hour basis, year after year—and also about finding, that is, *creating* dignity under those conditions. That counts, in my view, as a hard-won form of freedom.

Many of them read ravenously in those prison years; Palestinian activists often refer to the Israeli jail as the best Palestinian university. They read Mahatma Gandhi and Henry David Thoreau and biographies of Martin Luther King and Nelson Mandela—not that they needed those books to discover their own path to nonviolent resistance. *That* they learned from their own experience.

I have heard them speak of this at times, often in connection with a strong sense that freedom worthy of the name is always mutual and indivisible. Their freedom flows into and through mine and cannot be cut off from mine, as mine is intricately woven into theirs. By the same token, freedom of that order is not an element or component of something else, some larger complexity. You can't chop it into analytical pieces. Being indivisible, it naturally reaches toward any gap or blockage— toward freedom that has been stolen or denied. Thrust back, as it were, on itself, or on us, constricted as we are, the freedom we feel in Palestine thus carries with it sadness and sorrow.

9.

It comes down to a question of awareness and its specific qualities. Awareness is not the same thing as knowledge. Neville Symington rightly says, "Knowledge can be free from pain but awareness never."[14]

There is no dearth of pain in consequential freedom. Much human suffering precedes and follows it. The burst of freedom, while it lasts, washes away doubt and hatred, but it cannot in itself undermine the oppressive system that we confront in the occupied territories. Perhaps someday, if there are enough of these momentary bursts of being free that happen to ordinary people prepared to protest and take the risk, they will erode that system. In the meantime, one does what has to be done.

To feel free, in the limited way I have described, is probably an achievement. It has a price. Dostoyevsky stated the price better than anyone else ever has; here is his Grand Inquisitor addressing Christ:

"Instead of seizing men's freedom, You gave them even more of it! Have You forgotten that peace, and even death, is more attractive to man than the freedom of choice that derives from the knowledge of good and evil? There is nothing more alluring to man than freedom of conscience, but neither is there anything more agonizing. . . . Instead of ridding men of their freedom, You increased their freedom, and You imposed everlasting torment on man's soul."[15]

I've spent the last sixteen years or so in the company of ordinary people who have embraced the torment and taken the risk. I'm not by any means the only one who has been touched by, and in turn embraced, this odd sense of freedom. I think of my friend Eid Suleman al-Hathalin from Umm al-Khair, whom you've met. His moods vary and run the gamut from a reflective despair to a sort of wry hope. He doesn't complain. Ironically, it is the Israeli Occupation, in its tormenting injustice, that has set Eid free in the sense I'm getting at. The more they close him in, harass him, tear down his tent, steal his goats, threaten him with prison and expulsion, arrest his friends, attack his family, bully him verbally and physically, the freer he seems to be. His freedom, too, is contingent, remote from anything absolute or universal, entirely personal—not directly correlated with happiness, either. It has a pronounced quality of depth, of a gradually opening, steady space. It's a somewhat different way of saying no.

How do we recognize freedom of this kind when we meet it? We recognize it, unmistakably, because it preexists in us. We recognize it the way we recognize a Beethoven quartet as beautiful—because it takes our breath away, and because it steals up on us unawares, and because it is not devoid of pain, and because it is singularly unsentimental and antiheroic. What normally passes for the heroic is antithetical to this awareness, which has a reflective, or sober, quality and which may be actualized under conditions I have described.

But then I have to conclude, to my surprise, that what I have been talking about all along is not, after all, a sensation. The unfalsifiable sensation is but the surface manifestation of some facet of my being. Some unstructured space, accessed at times by saying "no" but regularly blocked to feeling, is apparently intrinsic to our being alive and, indeed, very close to us, to the tensile reality of our minds. It won't save us from dying, and I wouldn't want it to, but it's there. I am thus free without knowing it except in odd, irregular, unpredictable moments. But here I have to agree, again, with the Indian thinkers who tell us that it is our *lack* of awareness that is, in fact, truly the most precarious part of ourselves. Strange to say, many seemingly unimportant and accidental things will suffice to remedy the distress. One doesn't even have to resort to extreme measures like going to the South Hebron hills, as I, perhaps more occluded than most, have to do.

The particular conditions of South Hebron have taught me something crucial. Like truth in action—I will come back to this—becoming free means moving from relative constriction to an expansive mode of being. Such a movement is ethically charged. To impair the freedom of another being is to narrow one's own self to a rude and bitter thing. For an entire people to impair the freedom of another people is to multiply self-constriction exponentially; in just this way, Israel of the last five decades has become ill and narrow at heart. The only way we can heal ourselves now is to set the other free. When this happens, it will not be, in essence, a separation but rather a novel form of connectedness, beyond the operation of everyday causality. Something of that connectedness already exists: Israelis know that their fate is inseparable from that of Palestine, though they may not know that they know it, and they have deprived themselves of the freedom that would enable them to act on what they know.

10.
April 2, 2011, Susya, Twaneh, Beit Ummar

I wake at 5:00, enraged, for no special reason. Maybe it's just the relentless daily cumulation, the noxious blend of racism, hatred, and self-righteous nationalism that fills the public space in Israel these days. On Sunday I had to suffer through a speech by Netanyahu at the National Library. This is what he said: "We are the people of the Book. Our Book is *the* book, better than all other books. When it was translated into Greek, it immediately became clear to the Greeks that all existing Greek books could not compete with it and should be thrown away." I guess he was referring to Homer, Sophocles, and Plato. But this is a minor, almost trivial example.

So I'm very glad to be going down to South Hebron today—it's the least I can do. Last weekend was hard. Sixteen of our activists were arrested and spent over twenty-four hours in jail; when they were brought before a judge, he threw the case out of court and reprimanded the army for making illegal arrests and for interfering with the basic right to demonstrate. Much worse happened to Assaf, who was arrested—again illegally—in Silwan, in East Jerusalem; while handcuffed, sitting inside the police command car, the policemen sprayed him with pepper gas. I can tell you from experience that this isn't fun. It blinds you for a couple of hours or more, and it hurts like hell. They took him to the emergency room and released him toward nightfall.

In short, I'm expecting to be arrested today, and I'm at peace with this thought. We're a relatively large group, maybe thirty altogether, in two large transits. We take the back road to Susya, avoiding the Zif roadblock—as Yehuda says, "This is our own roadblock, just for peace activists, perhaps the only one in the territories meant for Israelis; it's rather nice to have a roadblock that is specially for you"—but this doesn't help in the end. Outside Susya, a vast flotilla of soldiers and policemen is waiting, probably more than I've ever seen at one time in the South Hebron hills. They pull us over. They tell us they're going to escort us to our destination. In a way, this development may not be a bad one: we're here today to block the settlers from grazing their sheep and goats in the fields of Susya and Twaneh, and it's possible that the soldiers, for all their clumsiness and their primary solidarity with the settlers, may end up helping us do just that. We take off, with the army vehicles right behind.

Soon we're in Susya, and within seconds—good timing—we get the report: Settlers are invading the Palestinian fields. We rush over the hilltop, past the tents and shacks and the wind generator that Noam and Elad installed, then down the slope, over rocks and thorns and a few forlorn patches of green barley, and up the next arid hill to where some ten or twelve settlers are screaming at the Palestinians and threatening them, as is their wont. It's a colorful scene: settlers in white, their enormous skullcaps and long fringes flapping in the wind, their docile, impassive sheep spreading over the hill; twenty or so Palestinians, men and women, in bright reds and blacks, taking their stand in what is left of their lands; the doomed barley tentatively, hopelessly poking up its gaunt shoots amid the dominant yellow-brown; a fierce midmorning spring sun reflecting off the white stones; brilliant blue spring skies; our activists with their backpacks and cameras and cell phones; and a drab set of soldiers now approaching, intent on separating the two rival parties. We have arrived just in time.

I know the ranking army commander in the field from my last visit, not long ago. He's not a bad man, but he's in a lousy mood this morning, barking out orders, trying desperately to get us to retreat back up the hill and to move the settlers and their flocks out of the wadi with its succulent thorns. He of course threatens to arrest us. Surprisingly, after a few minutes the settlers, under pressure, begin to move off to the south—but not before one of them rushes at us with his video camera, eager to record the faces of the Jewish traitors he despises. (Just last week one of the settler rabbis issued a legal ruling allowing Jews in the territories to use video cameras on Shabbat to photograph Palestinians and people like us.) "What's your name?" he asks me, camera rolling. I tell him. "What are you doing here?" "I'm here," I say to him, "to perform God's commandments." He's taken aback by the answer, and for one short, blessed moment there's a pause, a pregnant silence, as if thought had broken through a barrier.

We all know why we're here. In the interlude that ensues, Yehuda lucidly formulates the matter for the benefit of a foreign film team. "It is," he says, "the small things that are important. The real fight against the Occupation is happening here, in places like Susya. A very valuable, desperate kind of resistance

is going on. The soldiers will say to us, 'Why are you struggling over this miserable, dry field? What's the big deal? You're
here only to make a provocation.' But that is what the rich man
says, the man who can't understand the poor man's suffering.
These few fields are all that are left to the Palestinians in Susya,
and they are endangered. The settlers sit in their homes with
running water, plenty of food, soldiers to protect them, all
that they need, and the Palestinians are scraping a hand-to-
mouth existence out of their sheep and these few rocks and
thorns, under the settlers' guns. Every day they are in danger
of losing more land. We come here to help them. In this micro-
struggle, persistence counts. The moral act counts. Solidarity
counts. It's a game—a deadly game, but a nonviolent one on
our part—that we play with the soldiers and the settlers, and it
has its rules. What we see is that the Palestinian Authority has
accepted this form of struggle; they now know this is how we
must proceed. Salam Fayyad, the Palestinian Prime Minister,
was here in Susya last week."

"But why," asks the filmmaker, "do ordinary Israelis treat
the Occupation with such indifference, why don't they want to
change it?" It's a good question, one I have asked myself perhaps thousands of times. Yehuda answers: "There's a system in
place, and everything feeds it—the Ministry of Defense and the
Ministry of Internal Security and the Ministry of Agriculture
and the Treasury and the Army and the Police and the courts.
All are complicit. But beyond that, I think Israeli society has
become something like a sect. People unthinkingly follow what
their leader tells them to do, like sheep." 'Abed, a true shepherd, overhears and objects: "Not *my* sheep," he says. "They
think for themselves."

So already, by midmorning, we've had one minor victory;
the settlers have been briefly stopped in their tracks, at one tiny
point. They soon try their luck at another one, one hill over.

Amiel and his group of activists are waiting for them, and again the soldiers arrive, and this time they arrest the whole Ta'ayush group for infringing on a closed military zone. "You're not merely arrested," they scream at the activists, "you're 'exponentially' arrested." From our perch near the Susya tents, we ponder the wisdom of rushing over to join them; Amiel, speaking to us on the cell phone, says not to, they don't need any more detainees just now.

After an hour, we see a large group heading toward us—the soldiers have released Amiel and the rest, warning them that this is their "last and only chance" to obey orders. A second minor victory. Things are going well today. We say goodbye to our friends at Susya and drive north.

Maybe we'll be home before dark after all. Or will we? We stop on the way back at the small town of Beit Ummar, which has recently been sealed off entirely by the army as punishment, they say, for rocks thrown at cars on the main road. Two Palestinians from Beit Ummar were wounded two weeks ago when a settler opened fire. So now huge cement blocks embellish the main road in and out. We toy with the happy idea of somehow removing the middle one and reopening the road, but for all our pushing and tugging and chipping away at it, it won't budge. Meanwhile, two army jeeps full of soldiers have turned up, and they don't want us there. We decide that we'll at least stand at the entrance to the town and chant a few slogans, for the benefit of whoever might be listening. I should stress that such impromptu demonstrations by a handful of activists in open, public space are entirely legal—as a judge in Jerusalem confirmed last week. So we cry out into the void: "*End the Occupation now! The Occupation is a crime. From Beit Ummar to Bil'in, freedom freedom Palestine.*" And so on. Hardly a mighty chorus.

But the soldiers, with their stun grenades and tear gas and

combat vests and camouflage helmets, have by now lined up in front of us, and they seem both bewildered and very angry. They push us toward the metal barrier marking the start of Palestinian territory—Area B, in fact, though a huge red sign falsely warns that it is Area A and that it is a crime for Israelis to enter. I figure the stun grenades will start going off soon, and unfortunately I'm quickly proved right. We argue with the commander, we know we're well within the limits of the law, but of course it doesn't help; he declares we're in a Closed Military Zone, as usual, though in the confusion and tumult hardly anyone can see the signed order, if there is one, and then come the warnings: You have two minutes to leave, after that you'll be arrested. But they don't wait even two minutes, they're pounding us with their fists and twisting our arms and kicking at our groins, all of it gratuitous and unprovoked, and I hear one of them say: "Let's fire rubber bullets," and a stun grenade explodes nearby, and Amiel is hurled to the pavement, where he rolls over twice before coming to rest, apparently unscathed; he lies there calmly, smoking his cigarette, as the screams and curses and cries of pain and rage echo through space, and one of the soldiers simply loses it and pounces, like a wild beast, on Yehuda and roars into his ear, "Ahu Sharmuta, Ben Zonah," which is how you say "sonofabitch" in Arabized Hebrew slang, and so it goes for what seems like quite a long time.

I'm not one who gets into shouting matches with the soldiers. Also, violence sickens me. I'm not entirely sure why we have chosen this battlefield, not that it matters, and after all to a large extent it wasn't really our choice—just more of the occupation routine. But when they arrest Gil, and then Amiel, I can see there's another, pressing choice to be made: either we bundle the activists into the vans and leave, or we stay and get arrested, too. There's a certain sense to the former option, because the police are now here and they've swooped down on our Palestinian drivers, who are in real danger; we'd like to get them out of here. And there are some of the activists who can't or don't want to get arrested today. Time wears on. Conflicting instructions come in over the cell phones: Ezra says we should get the hell out, Amiel says we should stand our ground. I think it through. Where is my place? Where is the place of any good man or woman at such a moment? Then I know: I am not getting on that van. We send one party of activists and internationals off toward Jerusalem, and I turn back to the incredulous policeman who thought he was finally getting rid of us for today, and I say, easily, strangely joyful, calmly, "Arrest me now."

With me are another fourteen or so who are marched to the hideous, airless, armored arrest vehicle with its small slits for rifle fire that are now locked shut. One by one we are pushed inside. I have just enough time, a few seconds, to call Eileen on my cell phone before they handcuff me. She doesn't answer; I leave a message. "You should know," says the chief policeman, "that the village of Beit Ummar will pay tomorrow for what you've done today." I'm sure he's right: the only operative law in the occupied territories works just like that. They'll make them pay. Isa, wise, humane, naturally brave Isa, watches sadly from the hill as we disappear.

I recommend such moments, odd as this may sound. Really, there's nothing like it. Of course, the plastic handcuffs are too tight and my wrists hurt, and I'm thirsty and physically exhausted and I don't know how long I'll be like this and what will happen, but I'm with the salt of the earth, truly, and I can laugh, and recall previous arrests that I'm proud of, and there are other memories to be shared, and a burden has been lifted from my shoulders and a kind of sweet relief takes its place, and there's no fear but only a tense readiness or anticipation, and bits of texts or broken sentences flit through my mind; I've been reading Spinoza lately and some childish inner voice absurdly announces that Spinoza would approve. But actually what I mostly feel is simply, deeply alive, and strangely free, indeed far freer than I was before. Incongruous well-being mingles with minor bodily pain (after a while my wrists start to chafe and turn red). We wait.

Eventually they pick five from among us and drag them outside; they have been selected for a harsher fate than ours. The rest of us, still cuffed, are driven north at breakneck speed, with occasional sudden lurches of the brakes, past the checkpoint and the tunnels outside Jerusalem to the turn-off at Gilo, where we're rather unceremoniously dumped by the side of the road. Dolev is saddened by this rough-and-ready emancipation—nine others are still languishing in the Etzion or Kiryat Arba police stations. A cold wind is blowing, and the skies are heavy with cloud. There's a bus stop at this corner that we've named Ezra Nawi Junction, and there's even a large colored graffito on the wall that reads "We are all Ezra Nawi"—this from the day last year when Judge Elata Ziskind sent Ezra to jail for a month for doing the sorts of things we were doing today. The graffito has been painted over by an entirely sinister one: "Kahane was right." Meir Kahana—the prophet of Jewish racism and tribal hate.

Mostly settlers use this bus stop. I think someday when the nightmare is over, there will really and truly be a plaque or a small monument here in stone, in Hebrew and Arabic, in honor of Ezra and the nonviolent struggle he has led for the simplest, most basic right that all human beings own by virtue of being born. If no one else puts it up, we'll do it ourselves.

5

THIRST

May 24, 2008, Samu'a

Imagine a village on a brown rocky hill. A tractor, a few donkeys, a horse or two, a jumble of stone houses. Imagine the access road to the village, meant to connect up with the larger road that flows into the main north-south route from Jerusalem to Hebron. Imagine a tall mound of compacted earth and rock that blocks the access road completely—one of the 540-odd roadblocks that the Israeli army has put in place throughout the occupied West Bank. Ten meters to the south of the blocked road and parallel to it runs a dirt path that now serves the village; yellow taxis, minibuses, and private cars hobble along it to the point where it somehow impinges on the highway. So what is the point of the roadblock? That is one question.

Samu'a, like everywhere else in these parts, has a sad history. On November 13, 1966, a few months before the Six-Day War, an Israeli reprisal raid here killed three villagers and wounded ninety-six. The soldiers also destroyed a large piece of the village. One Israeli officer was killed. Samu'a had no connection whatsoever to the incident that set off the reprisal. Then came the war, partly set off, the experts say, by the raid. Did the raid serve any sensible purpose? That is another question.

Today we are going to take apart the roadblock with our bare hands and a shovel or two. We know it's a quixotic plan. Probably the soldiers won't let us achieve this goal; and even if we do succeed, the army will simply rebuild the barrier, reinforcing it this time with immovable concrete, within hours. All this is certain. Why, then, are we doing this? That question, at least, has an answer.

It is late morning by the time we turn up at the entrance to Samu'a. Some eighty or ninety villagers, young and old, are waiting, milling rather aimlessly around the blocked road that is lined on one side with ancient olive trees. We thought we would be joined by a large party from the Combatants for Peace, but we soon learn that the main bus of Combatants has been stopped by the police—who are, as always, well informed—at the Tunnels on Highway 60 near the southern edge of Jerusalem. Another busload coming north from Beer-Sheva was turned back by police at the Green Line, before they could enter Palestinian territory. That leaves us, one minibus full of Ta'ayush volunteers and observers, including my good friend Jyotirmaya Sharma from Hyderabad (on his first visit to Israel-Palestine) and Yael, a documentary filmmaker from Toronto. A small group of Combatants, young men and women led by Moshe Pesach, has somehow managed to make their way here by private cars. Ezra, the real hero of South Hebron, has brought along his nephew Shimon, just returned from a long trip to Australia; Shimon has never been in these hills and seems to have no clear idea of who is who out here in the Wild East. He knows there are settlers, and Palestinian villagers, and soldiers of various kinds, and policemen, but quite naturally he finds it difficult to make sense of the undecipherable jigsaw that presents itself to his fresh eyes. Why, he asks me, have they put this useless roadblock here? That question again.

The soldiers are, of course, waiting, too—a small row of reservists, as it turns out, perched on a ridge overlooking the battleground-to-be. They are, as usual, weighed down by their guns and tear-gas canisters and ammunition and who knows what else. That is one thing about soldiers: they are always carrying heavy things around, from one arbitrary point to another. This seems to be their true purpose in life; I remember it all too well. It is hot by now, and they are surely sweating in their uniforms and black boots. Some of them nonchalantly keep their guns trained on us. I wonder when their reinforcements will turn up. I wonder how much time we have.

Might as well begin. At first it is a simple enough matter of moving aside the surface rocks. The mound definitely looks capable of resisting our collective efforts: we poke at it, we kick it, we scrape away the top layers, but it is as if we have made no dent. After some time a pickax and a shovel or two appear. They help. It is pleasant working under the sun, side by side with the Samu'ans. At the same time, there are those familiar, insidious thoughts. Though I'm not fond of the symbolic, today's effort will, I know, be only that. Maybe "only" is not the right word.

Moshe, meanwhile, is addressing the soldiers—trying, I think, to ensure that they stay on their ridge and don't start shooting rubber bullets. "This is your chance," he says to them, patiently, calmly, slowly articulating the words so he can be sure they are heard. "You can meet real people today—the people you think you have the right to control, the people you don't allow yourselves to see. You think they're your enemies, but everyone here is devoted to peace. They just want to be free, and they will be free, and not through violence. Come down and talk to them. Listen to what they have to say." And so on. The soldiers look right through him. Beside him stands a Palestinian doctor from Halhul, not far down the main road, and he, too, has much to say to the soldiers. He speaks to them in English. "Someday you will put down those guns. You will take off those uniforms. You will come over to our side. You don't believe me, but I know that it is true. You will let your real nature, your goodness, come out. Then you will not understand how you could stand there, threatening me, today."

By now these soldiers are far from alone. An impressive array of police jeeps and armored vehicles have joined them; and we recognize the police officer who has arrived from Kiryat Arba to take command of this dangerous crisis. He is heavyset, heavy-jowled, short of stature, and mean; we know him from long experience in these parts. He takes the megaphone and barks at us, as is his wont: "What you are doing is illegal. Stop at once or face arrest."

Sometimes I wonder if they will ever realize that their threats only spur us on.

Amazingly, by now the once-large mound has been whittled down almost to ground level, but there is a major problem: an enormous boulder has been exposed, clearly the lynchpin of the whole foolish edifice, and it doesn't look like we can move it. Ropes are brought from the village; we tie them to the boulder, we line up along the length of the road and, at the signal, strain and pull together, but the stone won't budge. We try again and again, as the snarling from the direction of the soldiers becomes more raucous and insistent. I notice that a detachment from the Yasam—Israel's dark-clad riot police, not famous for their tender ways—has also pulled up beside the other military vehicles. I can guess what comes next.

First, however, we make one or two last-ditch attempts.

A tractor backs up toward what is left of the barrier, and the ropes circling the boulder are attached to it from behind. The tractor groans, tries to drag the rock away. The ropes slip off. We tie them again. They slip off again. I am not sure how many times this hopeful ritual is performed before the Yasam come rushing at us down the road, over the dirt we have dug away, over the stones, past the decapitated roadblock, toward the village. The Palestinians, familiar with such moments, retreat hastily toward their homes and the olive groves. For our part, we mostly melt away at the side of the road. So far, no one has been hurt.

Moshe tells me later that he was sure they were about to shoot; he could see their fingers itching at the triggers. Thankfully, something held them back today—the photographers perhaps? Who can say? These things don't look so good on the evening news. But at Saffuriyya in the Galilee, just ten days ago, the riot police ran amok, and many peaceful demonstrators were hurt. Maybe there is no rhyme or reason. I'm glad they didn't shoot.

This is not quite the end; the story twists back upon itself to allow a happy irony to emerge. Ezra has parked his big black car on the side of the main access road, far from the scene of conflict, close to the village, and taken off for some safe haven; he can't afford to get arrested. He has so many trials pending, an organic cumulation from years of active struggle to help the people of South Hebron, that a new arrest may land him in jail for long months. The keys to the car are, however, in the ignition, and innocent Shimon is sitting by the wheel. The police drag him from the car which, they now inform us, they intend to tow away—on the truly astonishing charge of obstructing the flow of traffic. I can only admire their ingenuity, since they are the ones who blocked this road in the first place with the barrier we have just dismantled. Let no one say the police of South Hebron are uncreative. Yet they may not notice the irony, for when Shimon asks them, with blank incomprehension, why they are taking away the keys, they pounce on him and arrest him, of all people. Amiel and Assaf try to intervene and are arrested as well, this time on the charge of obstructing a policeman who is discharging his duty. The three are carted off to the waiting vans, Shimon evidently horrified and confused. We can hear him asking them plaintively, over and over, "But what did I do wrong?"

Another good question. I guess it was a good day, as days go in the South Hebron hills. The internet news channels carried the story: a mixed group of Palestinians and Israelis took apart a roadblock near Samu‘a before the security forces charged and made arrests. Perhaps it seems a matter of little consequence, to say the least, something on the very edge of invisibility and beneath the threshold of meaning. And so it is. Perhaps it wasn't really worth the effort. When the Tel Aviv bus of the Combatants finally managed to get through, some hours later, the Yasam riot troops were still waiting for them; they made three more arrests and broke the arm of one young Israeli girl, a computer programmer who was taken to the hospital and then, with her new cast, to the Kiryat Arba jail. Ezra, lured by the purloined car keys to the same police station, was arrested as soon as he went in (that is what they wanted from the start); he spent the night there, until someone realized, in the morning, that they had no warrant to tow away his car after all. So he was sent home. He'll be back tomorrow or the next day, and we'll be coming back, too.

Some risks are worth taking, but it's better not to ask why. Then there are the risks that you *have* to take if you want to feel human. Perhaps one of those children from the village who watched us pulling at the rope, Jews and Arabs, young and old, men and women, before the soldiers charged, will remember this day, and the memory will change his life. I know Jyotirmaya won't forget: a Gandhian moment in the middle of nowhere, with no obvious results—all the better for that. A dusty sweetness infused the day. Maybe our doctor friend is right, and eventually the soldiers will put down their guns. After all, every one of the Combatants for Peace used to carry one, and look where they are today. I'm sure the roadblock is back by now, the village taxis are creaking over the parallel dirt track beside the olive trees, the shepherds have been attacked again, the settlers have stolen another Palestinian field or two, and some imbecile of an officer, even as I write, is sitting in his headquarters happily planning another raid.

May 3, 2009: Pogrom at Khirbet Safa

Pogroms: it's something the Jews know about. I grew up on those stories—Cossack raids on the *shtetl,* the torture and killings and wanton destruction. My grandmother had a brother. They lived in Mikhalayev, in the Ukraine. One day the Cossacks came, and everyone panicked; the seventeen-year-old brother tried to hide in a pond, and he drowned. She mourned that young death all her life; the dead don't age, and some wounds never heal.

And now it turns out—who would believe it?—that there are Jews who also know how to carry out pogroms. For the last ten days or so, settlers from Bat 'Ayin in the so-called Etzion Bloc have been paying violent daily visits to their Palestinian neighbors in Khirbet Safa, perched high on the edge of the western ridge that overlooks the coastal plain all the way to the sea.

A terrorist from Khirbet Safa entered Bat 'Ayin two weeks ago, murdered a settler boy with an ax, and wounded another. The police caught him soon thereafter. But that hasn't stopped the Bat 'Ayin settlers from repeated rampages to wreak revenge on Khirbet Safa. According to the villagers at nearby Beit Ummar (unconfirmed by other sources), there have been heavy casualties in Khirbet Safa—some eleven or twelve wounded, some severely, by gunfire. As if that weren't bad enough, the soldiers have apparently been making common cause with these settlers, opening fire readily at the villagers. Life in this most lovely of the mountain villages has become a nightmare; not that it was easy before.

We get the emergency call around 5:00 after a long day that started off in Susya, in South Hebron. At first it looked as though we'd never get through the barriers and the roadblocks. Two full buses and several private cars headed south by the long route twisting over the dry hills. A gray, sultry day, summer approaching: in the endless battle in the wadis and terraces between green and brown, green seems to be losing ground. Every once in a while the soldiers would stop one of the cars and threaten to stop the buses. But, happily, by midday we had rendezvoused at Susya with a van of Palestinian activists from all over the West Bank. All in all, some 150 Combatants for Peace had come to meet each other and to see the reality of South Hebron.

This is what it will look like one day, I was thinking. Like in Berlin when the Wall fell. Maybe I won't live to see it, but I know it will be like this. People, ordinary people from both sides, pour out of the vehicles more or less into one another's arms. The soldiers in their jeeps with their guns and other deadly toys are helpless to hold back this flood of dangerous fraternization. Some of them look to me like they'd like to join us. It all happens fast and very naturally, without thinking. Walking over the rocks and thistles toward the tents of Susya, I hear snippets of conversation like many I've heard before. Awkward, tentative, eager. Strangers introduce themselves: "I'm 'Abed. I live in the refugee camp at Dahariyya." "We're from Bethlehem." "I'm from Tel Aviv, I'm a student. I served in the fucking army for three and a half years." (This with a somewhat sheepish smile). A young Palestinian man to a dark-haired Israeli woman: "Would you come visit me in my home some day?" "I don't know. Maybe. I'm afraid." A short silence. "Yes, I'll be happy to come." I, too, embrace my friends: Hafez, Isa, Nasser, Eid. The gentle, irrationally hopeful, anxious Eid.

We stand among the black tents facing the Israeli settlement of Susya with its red-tile roofs and the new "illegal outpost" that settlers have put up on the next hill, just a couple of hundred meters off. In the distance, at Shuneran, you can see the lonely white whirl of the new turbine our people have recently set up for our Palestinian friends. Wind-driven, it's already generating enough power to run a refrigerator and a newfangled butter-and-cheese churn: the milk goes into the drum of an old washing machine that shakes it wildly up and down, and in practically no time there is the unlikely miracle of butter. Just two weeks ago I watched Bedouin women doing it the old way, in a goatskin hung over a fire and rocked back and forth for long hours. This turbine at Shuneran is like a gift from the gods.

Ofra, wiry, battle-worn, lucid, is speaking to the crowd as Yusri translates into Arabic: "The Occupation has an interest in preventing us from meeting one another, and an even greater interest in preventing us from struggling together. But we will never allow them to separate us. This is our responsibility and our answer to apartheid. We had to get past the barriers and roadblocks to come here today, and we also had to break through the metaphorical walls that have divided us." I wonder how Yusri is going to manage this last sentence. He lives in a world of very real walls and barriers. But no, he's got it, no problem: "*hawajiz majaziyeh*—that is," he explains, "the walls that have been erected in our minds."

Still, it looks like today is going to be rather bland. There are the dialogue sessions that take time—many of the Israeli Combatants have never been in South Hebron or anywhere else in the territories, and some are meeting living people from the other side for the first time. The seasoned few of us from Ta'ayush wait, a little bored. The truth is we're having trouble holding ourselves back from what our instincts tell us is the thing to do—that is, from marching the whole crowd up the hill toward the new outpost. It's not every day you get 150 activists here in Susya. But there's been a decision: no confrontations today. You can't expose the first-timers to the whole terror and rigor of the Occupation. And yet that hill is so enticing. There's a new settler caravan in place, too. All we have to do is to start walking. . . .

And then, surprisingly, a new decision crystallizes. We will "take" that hill after all. We'll follow Nasser up to the ancient well that belongs to the Hadari-Hareini families but that is now off limits to them; the settlers won't let them near it. In South Hebron, a well means the difference between life and death. We head out over the rocky terraces. Movement, at last, and action: the relief is sweet and viscous as a heady liqueur. My lungs take in the sharp smell of wild sage, thyme, and the aromatic herb the Palestinians call *Amaslimaniya*, said to heal infections and stomach pains. I wonder if it heals heartache, too. The very fragrance seems to be healing mine.

We reach the well, and Nasser finds the black leather bucket and lowers it deep into the bowels of the earth and draws up fresh spring water, the sweetest water in the world; he pours it into our bottles and canteens and straight into our mouths, he is smiling as if entranced, drunk on the water of his own well, soaked to the skin, and for that brief unforgettable minute or two the world seems almost right again. And then, of course, the soldiers swoop down on us, with some settler barking orders at them, and the officer flashes the inevitable piece of paper that declares we are in a Closed Military Zone and we have two minutes to get out before they start hitting us with their clubs and rifle butts and making arrests. The rightful owner of the precious well is driven off, again. The thief who has stolen the well stands beside it together with a small army of soldiers, with their perfectly legal slip of paper, to make sure he gets to keep it.

We have promised the Combatants that we won't get into any kind of tussle, so slowly—but still almost triumphant—we begin to withdraw. Take it as an object lesson, I say to Amit. This is how it works. Amit, new to this landscape, a doctoral student in philosophy, specialist in Husserl, is incredulous, not for the last time today. Don't worry, I say; we will yet turn the tide. As we walk, Joseph, a stalwart of South Hebron weekends, tells us about the organization called *Nefesh be-nefesh*, "Soul for Soul," run by two rabbis in Miami and supported by the Christian Zionist right; they paid him $4,000 to come to live in Israel, and they promised him another $4,000 if he'd make his home in one of the settlements in the territories. "I wonder," he says, "if Palestinian Susya would count."

By now our appetite has been whetted, and Amiel and Ezra decide that our small Ta'ayush squad will pay a visit, on our way home, to the plot of land that settlers near Hebron have recently stolen from the Ja'abar family; these settlers have put up a small, ugly shack on the land, with a "porch" canopied by brown camouflage net. Last week the army chased them off, because of our pressure, but they came back, of course, within a few hours. So we head north in the Palestinian van with Isa, and at some point along the highway we get out and make our way through desiccated vineyards and fallow fields uphill to the Ja'abars and then on to the hilltop and its hut. Some eight or nine settler teenagers in Sabbath white are sitting there, looking rather weary. Our arrival jogs them awake, and a messenger is sent to bring reinforcements; soon some older ones turn up, including a long-haired, wild-eyed boy-man caressing his M-16, his finger on the trigger and the clip loaded inside. He's crazy, Amiel says, be careful. We stare him down. Amit tries to talk to them—I think he'd like to persuade them by reasoned argument that what they're doing is immoral—with the usual result. I'm not sure how long the stalemate would have continued if we hadn't got the call from Isa: settlers are shooting in the village of Khirbet Safa; come at once.

We rush back to the van and race north, turning west at Beit Ummar. At once we're in the heart of Palestine. The roads are riddled with potholes, we pass donkeys and horses and rather a lot of goats and olive trees and ragged children. After a while we see that people are standing on their flat rooftops, apparently watching the battle going on in the village below them. And the first noises impinge upon us—the distant drumming of the guns. I am wondering what we're supposed to do. And what if we get caught between rock-throwing village teenagers and trigger-happy soldiers? Many have been shot here in the last few days. Some nervous thoughts flit through my brain, I think of my grandchildren, and Eileen, what am I doing here, then I remember my grand-uncle, drowned at seventeen. If only some decent person had been there to help. My head clears. Like any battlefield, this one is confusing; it takes some time, as we proceed into the village, to figure out who is doing what to whom. But half a kilometer or so away we see the army jeeps and half-tracks, and there are also soldiers standing near a wire fence with guns shouldered, as if to provide cover for the settlers. Two blue jeeps of Border Police turn up beside us on the road, and more soldiers jump out and take up their positions, focusing their telescopic sights.

Then it really begins. First the stun grenades, then the rubber-coated bullets—the Palestinians know each lethal genus and genre by the sound—then live bullets, lots of them. *Crack crack crack*—and the horrible hollow echo each time, as if the shot had turned back on itself and was searching for any soft, vulnerable surface. We take shelter on the porch of a new stone house by the roadside. There are several women draped in black, and a younger one, elegantly dressed, with a baby cradled in a blanket in her arms. I count seven young children. One of the older women is trembling and crying; I wish I could comfort her or calm her. Isa Sleby, gallant Isa, with his weak heart, too full of feeling, smiles calmly. He's another one of God's miracles, Isa, a man of principle, totally committed to nonviolent action, never afraid, never too tired to notice the fear or pain of those around him. Then there's our driver, who says to me, philosophically, "It's a good lesson. This is how things are, most days. It's a lesson in politics, or in war, in war as a part of politics." In the midst of it all, the women, intent on caring for their guests under any circumstances, serve tiny cups of Turkish coffee. Minutes pass to the accompaniment of intermittent rifle fire. The white-and-beige goats next door are furiously chewing away at the thorny shrubs in the yard, heedless of the vast ruckus just outside the gate.

Slowly we piece together from the villagers the story of this afternoon. First the settlers from Bat 'Ayin came in, shooting their guns. Some of the young men from the village tried to fight back, to protect their homes and families with whatever they had, and all they had was rocks. Then the soldiers arrived to save the settlers and started shooting, and the rock-throwing intensified. This is one way to reconstruct the sequence. By now it hardly matters. The only question is how to stop it.

I hear wailing and screaming from somewhere to my right, amid the olive trees and terraces, and then Amiel is calling me to come quickly; I was trained as a combat medic, and someone has been hit. I set off running in the direction of the screams, through the trees behind the houses, trying at the same time to find in my shoulder-bag the small set of pads and bandages and the rubber elastic to use as a tourniquet that I always bring along with me to South Hebron. It's been almost exactly 27 years, I quickly calculate, since I last ran like this to a wounded man, in the first Lebanon war; and God only knows if I'll remember what to do. They always used to tell us that the knowledge is buried in your fingers and will reemerge automatically when you need it. I hope they're right. In any case, there's no time to think. The wailing intensifies. Suddenly they're waving to me to turn back; an ambulance has found its way over the hill and driven off with the victim. Later we hear that he's wounded "moderately." Could have been worse.

And then we're back on the street standing right under the soldiers, and stray rocks are crashing down near us, and one of the young student girls who came with us is hit in the leg. She's a little shaken. A Palestinian woman needs to get home, perhaps she's worried about her children, she's afraid to climb the hill alone, so we envelop her on all sides and walk her uphill past the soldiers, who yell at us and try to stop us, but we ignore them and keep walking, and maybe after all we're finally having some effect on them because at last they hold their fire. Slowly, tentatively, painfully, a certain quiet sinks in as evening comes on and the hills turn purple and then black. As so often, Ezra materializes suddenly, just where he is needed; how he got here through all the chaos I will never know, but he is all smiles and he says to us, "You should know that it's only because we're here that they've stopped shooting." He stops in the street to remonstrate with the young rock-throwers. If only they would learn not to do that. He thinks someday they will learn.

It's hard to find a good man or a good woman, but I've been lucky in this respect. In fact, I've surrounded myself with them. As we walk back toward the van, Amit, the philosopher, tells me that this whole business just doesn't make sense. Why doesn't the army demolish the rickety hut those settlers have put up on the Ja'abar family's land? For that matter, why does the State of Israel send its soldiers to protect the settlers in the first place? And what was the point of shooting live bullets at the village once the settlers had been scuttled away? What's there to be gained from it? Everything seems to him surreal. He's right. A Jewish pogrom *is* surreal. He's learning Greek, and they've just started reading Plato's *Apology* in class. I remember that joy. For a passing second I can hear Socrates speaking to the settlers, who would undoubtedly have been all too happy to condemn him to die—who would probably have shot him outright: "Don't think that by killing someone you can escape being blamed for your own wickedness; that is neither possible nor honorable. . . . Wherefore, O judges, be of good cheer about death, and know of a certainty, that no evil can happen to a good man, either in life or after death. He and his are not neglected by the gods."

September 26, 2009, Jinbah, Water Convoy

Water—or rather the denial of water—is a potent weapon. Here in the arid South Hebron hills, it may be the most potent of all. Without water no one can survive here more than a few hours.

In the old days, before the Israeli Occupation, the Palestinians scattered over these hills in caves and tiny *khirbehs* survived on their wells and reservoirs. By now they've lost a great many of the wells, some poisoned or stopped up or simply taken over by Israeli settlers, others filled with rocks and sand by the army during violent raids on the *khirbeh*s in the late 1990s and after. These days some water—not nearly enough—is brought in on a daily basis, more or less, by tankers that wind their way laboriously over the goat paths. The main access route to Jinbah, a rough, rocky track that eventually links up with the main highway and the town of Yata, has been sealed off by the army— blocked, in fact, at twenty-three separate points by piles of rock and earth, or cut and rendered impassable where it meets a culvert. No trucks, no buses, no private cars can get around these obstacles, which the army puts in place, and sometimes removes, for no apparent reason.

It's expensive to bring in water by tanker to a place like Jinbah, a remote confabulation of black tents, stone goat pens, and ruined caves. According to my friend Eid, prices are pitched at between 150 and 200 Israeli shekels (roughly $40 to $50) just for hiring the tanker and the driver—a vast sum for these herders and peasant farmers—not including the water. One tankerfull won't last them more than a few days. If the old track were open, costs would be cut in half. We intend to open it today.

Why, you might ask, has the army closed the track in the first place? The standard excuse, which we hear from the soldiers at various moments through this day, is that they're fighting terrorism. They're always doing that, even in the absence of any living terrorists anywhere nearby. The only violence of note that afflicts the South Hebron hills comes from Israeli settlers. So maybe there's another reason. Maybe they want to dry up the Palestinian civilian population in this area—that is, to drive them from their homes. For our part, we're determined to help keep them on their land. That's why we're here today.

As usual, the police and army aren't too happy about our arrival. They dog our steps repeatedly as we make our way south with two busloads of activists, some hundred people in all. At the main turn-off to Umm Daraj, the road that will connect us to the water tankers and tractors already waiting for us deep in the desert, the soldiers are ready: several command cars, police vans and other vehicles, some officers, the standard gray-olive flotilla. Do they really think they can turn us back? We pour out of the buses and start walking rapidly up the road. You can see at a glance that we're too many for them, they can't possibly arrest us all, and they can't stop us. Soon we have left them far behind.

It's almost 11:00 in the morning and already very hot and getting hotter, and since we had to abandon our buses because of the soldiers we have a long walk past a few homes and pens for the flocks and then over the stark golden-white hills, down and up and down again. Soon we are alone in the desert, far from human habitation. The hills sweep and swirl almost as far as the eye can see; near the horizon, barely visible in the blinding light, a slight blue patch of the Dead Sea shimmers and hides, too vibrant to be real. After thirty or forty minutes, at the end of the road, the end of the world, tractors are waiting with attached metal-and-wood carts—called "platforms" in Hebrew—to carry us still deeper in, to the glowing, desolate point where the heavy tankers are parked.

Maybe it's a mirage. I almost rub my eyes. How they did get here? I'm not used to such precision planning. Soon the caravan departs. Groaning and creaking and jiggling and shaking, veering madly from side to side, always threatening to overturn, the tractors, with tankers and platforms attached, crawl over the rocks and plow through thick layers of dust and sand. It's a long, punishing, breathtaking ride, and just when I start to feel I can't stand much more of it, we grind to a halt on a rise overlooking a steep stony descent into the wadi. Here the track has been cut. We jump down from the platforms, mill around aimlessly for a while, unsure of what should happen next. Suddenly I find Eid, and we embrace. I haven't seen him for some weeks. How's life? Hard, as always. New houses are going up in the veteran settlement of Carmel, next to Umm al-Khair where Eid lives. So much for Obama's settlement freeze. The Palestinian shacks demolished some months back by the Occupation authorities have not been rebuilt. There's no money, and no hope. Aside from that, Eid says, if you don't identify yourself openly with one of the factions, Fatah or Hamas for example, the Palestinian Authority is likely to fire you from your job. It recently happened with about forty teachers. So it's very hard to find work. The good news is that his little daughter is starting to walk. He smiles, shy with happiness.

A yellow backhoe goes into action on the slope, smoothing down what's left of the narrow track. We race down the hill to help with this rebuilding of the route; we search for heavy boulders to fill the wide gap on either side of the culvert. There is no dearth of boulders. It's hard on the back and, like much physical labor in the South Hebron hills, strangely satisfying. Finally the backhoe rolls back and forth over the newly filled piece of track, compacting rock and dust, turning it into something akin to a road. Victorious, the backhoe moves on, and the water tankers now slowly creep down the hill and pass us on their way to Jinbah. I feel like cheering, and I can see I'm not alone.

The black tents of Jinbah are clearly visible on the hill above us to our left. Can people really live out here in this luminous wasteland? And assuming that the answer is yes, who in his right mind would want to drive them off, to starve them of water? At least, I say to myself, water is now on its way. But this, of course, is the moment the soldiers decide to turn up, eager to harass us. Possibly they want revenge for their failure to stop us at the turnoff. A heavy command car swoops down on us and heads straight for the backhoe. It's immediately clear they need a victim, and they've chosen the Palestinian driver; equally clear that we have to prevent his arrest. We converge from all sides on the backhoe. There's some shouting and arguing as the soldiers circle the machine, trying to reach the driver's cabin. We're too quick for them. I find myself climbing up, with Amiel and Assaf, to sit in the driver's seat, while the driver himself is swiftly helped down into the protective crowd and then manages to slip away.

OK, I have to confess. I always wanted to drive one of these things. I don't have a clue how to do it, but I like sitting there, peering down at the ruckus below, inspecting the many mysterious levers and gears. I could easily go on playing like this for some time, like my grandson Inbali when you put him behind the driver's wheel. I feel Assaf sliding something metallic and small into the pocket of my trousers: the ignition key. The soldiers mustn't find out that we still have the key, lest they impound the vehicle and drive it off to their base. That would be a true disaster: the owner of the backhoe needs it every day, his livelihood depends on it and, once confiscated, the machine is all too likely to be parked in the army camp for four to eight weeks, as in previous cases we can remember. We are going to have to stay here to guard the machine. The soldiers, meanwhile, are angry and frustrated, since their prey has eluded them. They prowl around the backhoe, they bark and snarl. They must be hot: it's midday, and they're loaded down with an entire armory, machine guns with grenade propellers, helmets, clips, and plenty of tear-gas canisters of different sizes and colors belted the whole length of their legs.

Maybe it's the relief that the driver is safe, or the satisfaction we felt when the water tankers chugged by on their way to Jinbah, or maybe it's the rage we feel because these soldiers have now announced to us that, by opening the track, we have committed a grave crime and will be punished. Maybe it's just a passing whim. Anyway, suddenly the desert air is resounding with the old cry of noble souls committed to doomed causes: *No pasaran!* "They—the Fascists—will not pass here." I know it doesn't sound likely, but nothing is likely in South Hebron. I'm shouting, too. *No pasaran!* It's a little silly. Anyway, I'm really glad there are people here who remember what it means and who see the parallel. But our Palestinian friends are, for once, bewildered. What *do* these words signify? In my rusty Arabic, in the middle of all the hubbub, immersed in dust and sun, I try to explain, a two-minute historical synopsis: once, in Spain, there was a civil war between the Fascists and people like us, who believe in freedom. . . . .The older ones pass down my explanation to the children, there are many young children with us here today, and now they are calling it out with us, and maybe this time it will come true.

But clearly our plans are in some danger. There's all that water to be poured into the Jinbah reservoir, and there are four more *khirbehs* to the east and west waiting to receive their allotment. We're needed there. So the main body of activists heads off to the Jinbah encampment, leaving ten or twelve of us to guard the backhoe with the soldiers for company.

I had a liter and a half of mineral water with me, but at the height of the mini-confrontation I handed the bottle around and it came back empty. It's not clear how long we're going to have to wait things out. We make a quick inventory of our water reserves. They're dangerously low. It's another one of those South Hebron scenes. Here we are, stranded in the middle of the desert in and around a backhoe that we can't abandon, with no driver anywhere near but also nowhere to go, with minimal water supply, and with a jeep full of grumpy and disoriented soldiers glowering at us. They also have no idea what to do or even, for the most part, why they are there, as we discover when we begin to engage them in conversation. Perhaps they have orders to wait here in ambush for the missing driver, who will sooner or later come back to reclaim his vehicle.

The standoff is complete: neither side can budge from its position. It feels like a perfect condensation of the general standoff in Palestine-Israel: terminal stasis, mental gridlock, and no workable exit strategy. I confer with Amiel. He says he, too, can't imagine how this will end. All we can do is wait. I tell my friend Istvan, who has joined us today for the first time, that on the basis of past experience I can predict that at some point everyone will just get tired and go home, but I can't guess when this might happen. It could take hours. Istvan is in no hurry. He has brought along his Hebrew textbook, and we spend a while discussing the odd fate of vowels in Hebrew and Greek—the perfect topic for such occasions. If only I weren't so thirsty. . . .

Suddenly, an apparition. Ezra, magically materializing out of thin air, pulls up in his car together with a tall, older man, perhaps eighty years old, who has something to say to the soldiers. His name is Benny Gefen, from Kabri in the Galilee. He doesn't waste words. In a deep voice, crisp with anger, he says to them: "For five years I served in the Palmach [the elite army before and during the 1948 war]. For twenty-nine years I did reserve duty in the paratroopers. My son was killed in the

Golani reconnaissance unit on the Lebanese border. I want to tell you that today I am ashamed of the uniform I used to wear, the uniform you are wearing now. In the Palmach they always taught us: think of what the other is feeling, put yourself in his place. But you don't care what happens to the Palestinians. You deny them water, the most basic of all human needs, and you back up the settlers, who terrorize them every day. I'm ashamed." He turns away without another word, goes back to the car, disappears, as if a Biblical prophet had wandered by for a moment and spoken from the bitterness of his heart. The soldiers, for the first time today, look a little nonplussed; one of them even, to my amazement and delight, appears to hang his head in shame.

After a while the soldiers clamber into their vehicle and drive away. This is our chance. We prepare to turn on the ignition and take off into the desert in the backhoe, a dozen Ta'ayush activists and five or six Palestinian children flying toward freedom in the empty spaces as if we were in some black-comic action film. I rather like the idea. But we're a minute or two too slow (none of us has driven a backhoe before), and suddenly a new jeep full of soldiers comes bouncing over the rocks and takes its position on the hilltop above us. Too late. Stalemate resumes. We hear on the cell phones that the main group of activists has been stopped by the army just as they were about to move out to the other sites, and that the inevitable order declaring the whole area a Closed Military Zone has been issued. Clearly, a water convoy is a serious provocation. Later it turns out that Benny Gefen emerged from the desert and delivered his sharp rebuke to the commanding officer there, too, and the officer, faced with so unequivocal a moral authority, had no choice but to back down.

Time passes, baked brittle, until at last we see one large

party of our friends coming back to us, snaking over the track, and now the solution reveals itself: we will envelop the back-hoe on all sides and walk it past the soldiers (a driver has help-fully turned up); we will prevent them, by sheer numbers, from getting anywhere near it. It works like a charm. And though the military jeeps keep tailing us over the hills, soon we are back on a rickety platform tied to a tractor with two (not three) good wheels, jolting our way painfully and slowly over the rocks in the direction of the main road. Still thirsty: it's important on a day like this to taste the torment of thirst in the desert. A good day's work. Maybe it does people good to taste the surreal—more real than anything real—from time to time. Maybe years from now one of those soldiers will remember Benny Gefen's words, and they will change his life. Maybe not all has been lost. *No pasaran.*

Our buses are ready to take us back the city, but there's one last scene in store. At the Al-Khadr terminal-checkpoint just south of Jerusalem, a young soldier comes aboard to check us out. "Where are you coming from?" he asks. From South Hebron. He scowls. "Jewish leftists. . . . Pull over." He's invented a new category, a rather ugly one. There are, in his mind, good Jews (settlers and the like, and your run-of-the-mill paranoid nationalists), there are (uniformly bad) Palestinians, and there are, it now turns out, also bad Jews like us. Leftists. He wants to detain us. This is too much for Yehuda, who leaps from the bus in search of the soldier's command-ing officer. He's determined to lodge a complaint. The soldier refuses to give his name and serial number, as the law requires, and by now he's lost it, curses Yehuda, who responds with vol-canic invective, and the verbal battle immediately spills over the huge terminal, back and forth, cameras clicking, activists swarming from the bus, until finally the commanding officer happens by—a burly young Border Policeman, eager to calm things down and get the damned bus out of the terminal. He surprises us. "Why are you so upset?" he asks Yehuda, disingenuous. "So what if he called you Jewish leftists? Aren't you proud of who you are? I'm a leftist myself, and proud of it, too."

January 16, 2010, Mufagara, Bi'r al-'Id, Tuba

Ziad Muhammad Yusuf Muhamra, from Bi'r al-'Id: sun-dried face, deep scars, lively eyes. It is hard for me to understand his Arabic, not only because it's fast, slurred, and in South Hebron dialect. He was shot in the throat by a soldier in 1986 while he, Ziad, was sitting on the ground; the bullet exited near his right nostril. Miraculously, he survived, but his speech was affected, and there was considerable damage to the nerves in his neck. I ask him to tell his story, and out it comes in a rush in the blinding midwinter sunlight as the sheep chew vigorously on thorns and greens around us.

"I was out with the sheep near Jinbah. They [the soldiers] chased us away. We fled back up the hills. Then the Green Patrol claimed we had crossed the Green Line into Israel, and they threatened us, and the settlers came down on us from above. They came at us from three sides, hemming us into the wadi with the sheep. I was with my brothers and my uncle. There were soldiers with guns and two men from the Shabak [General Security Services], Marko and Koby; we knew Koby well—he was often in the area. First Marko hit me hard, a fight broke out, an inspector from the Green Patrol was wounded on his ear. They told us we had to leave. I sat down on the ground and covered my head with my arms. The soldier gave me a heavy blow with the butt of his gun. One of the soldiers took out a pistol. I could hear him playing with the clip. They said they'd shoot me if I didn't get up and go away, but I just sat there. I wasn't going to leave my lands, so the soldier shot me here [pointing to the scar on his neck]. Afterward when I was lying there bleeding I heard Koby and the soldier concocting their story. They said they'd report that I'd tried to grab a weapon, so they shot me. But they were worried. Finally they called a helicopter that took me to Soroka Hospital in Beer-Sheva. I was in the hospital for a long time. At first I couldn't talk and I couldn't eat; they fed me through a tube directly into my stomach for a whole year. For months I saw the doctors. There was a doctor in Bellinson and another in Shaarei Tzedek who tried hard to help me. On the day I was finally able to eat solid food again—a banana—the whole ward crowded around me, nurses, doctors, everyone; some were crying from joy. The authorities demanded that I pay a fantastic sum for the medical expenses, but anyway we have no money. In the end, the army paid. The day after I was shot the army arrested my two brothers and held them for a month."

Ezra says: "Here's a story with a half-happy ending." "Half?" I say. "Yes, he's still alive, he can talk, he has a life." He's not alone. On the way here we see Khalid, shot in the stomach by settlers at the time of the first Iraq war. He's alive, so it's another half-happy story.

June 26, 2010, Bi'r al-'Id

There's a strange allure in the viscous black mud that comes up from the depths of the earth, from the bottom, or somewhere near the bottom, of the well we are cleaning in Bi'r al-'Id. Bucket after bucket of it, lifted by pulley from down below, straggles to the surface, where we unload it and pour it out on the rocky escarpment. Its texture changes remarkably over the long morning hours from a watery top layer to heavy, shiny dark loam to a granular, sticky brown. It has a strong smell, like the sulphurous mud from the Dead Sea (not very far away) that people smear over their bodies for healing. Yehuda says the Palestinians of Bi'r al-'Id should bottle it and sell it at the airport: "Sacred Mud from the Sacred Desert." There's no end to it. The buckets go down and up, down and up, heavier each time; the rope attached to the pulley is now caked solid with mud, and the escarpment has turned into a mire. Amiel, Dolev, and Danny are down in the dark recesses, filling the buckets alongside Haj Isma'il. Suddenly Ezra arrives—he was released from jail only a few days ago—and immediately lowers himself, like Spider Man, down the shaft. You can't stop him. When they emerge hours later, they are black troglodytes, covered with mud from head to toe; and we, too, working the buckets above ground, are splattered, encrusted, soaked.

When I said goodbye to Amiel almost five months ago, he said, "We will meet in the spring, and when you get back, things will be the same here, just a little worse." But actually in some ways they're a lot worse. The continuing struggles against the Occupation, on the ground in the territories, take their usual grim course, but inside Israel hardly a day passes without some new and sickening jolt. The country is in the grip of violent nationalist paranoia spiked with inventive forms of wickedness and active hatred for Palestinians, of an intensity I've never seen before. Here, for example, is what Yulia Shalamov Berkovitch, a member of the Knesset (from the Kadima "centrist" party), has to say: "'Israeli academia apparently suffers from 'Palestinomania,' a mild psychological illness whose symptoms include self-hatred, an affinity for Israel's enemies,

Jewish anti-Semitism and/or anti-Zionism. The spread of 'Palestinomania' demands immediate and painful treatment for all of our sake, and the sooner the better" (*Haaretz,* June 21). I wonder what treatment she has in mind: Lobotomies? Re-education camps? Firing squads? In the same report, we learned that the Minister of Education, Gideon Sa'ar, thinks that it is "important to examine the issues" raised by a rabidly right-wing group called Im Tirtzu in a report on "anti-Zionist trends" in Israeli universities. According to Im Tirtzu, 80 percent of the reading materials assigned in the departments of political science in Israel are anti-Zionist and anti-nationalist and should, one must assume, be banned. They seem to have a black list; the next step, I suppose, is censorship in the classroom, followed by book burnings in the public square.

Milder signs of the times are everywhere; the mayor of Ramat Hasharon in the coastal plain has decreed that in all schools that require a uniform, the pupils, from next year on, will have to tie Israeli flags to their wrists. He must feel, perversely, that a lack of patriotism is eating away at the foundations of our national existence. Add to this the decision by Jerusalem's mayor Barkat to demolish twenty-two Palestinian houses in Silwan—the same homes we saved by an international campaign in 2005—and the ongoing, indeed escalating evictions of Palestinian families from their homes in Sheikh Jarrah. Barkat seems intent on setting the city on fire.

But here we are in Bi'r al-'Id, where our Palestinian hosts are, miraculously, rebuilding the homes from which they were cruelly evicted over a decade ago. The sun is dancing, the wind fierce for a summer day, the sky endlessly open like the desert stretching toward the horizon just below us. I ask my friend Muhammad how things have been during my absence. "Fine," he says; "no problems." Afterward I hear that his father was recently assaulted by Yaakov Talya, the notorious settler-owner of the ranch aptly named Lucifer's Farm, hardly half a mile away; when the soldiers turned up, they of course arrested Muhammad's father. He is now awaiting trial. (Perhaps the military judges will send him to jail for the crime of having been attacked, as they have so many others we know.) And the road to Jinbah, which we can see from our perch on the high ridge, has again been closed by the army after we punched it open with a water convoy last fall. Not long ago a boy from Jinbah was seriously injured and had to be carried all the way up the mountain to the road near Bi'r al-'Id. Two weeks ago settlers from Chavat Maon entered Palestinian Twaneh, threw rocks at the villagers, and tried to set a Palestinian house on fire. In short: *Plus ça change.* . . .

I have missed these weekends in South Hebron—missed the people, the Arabic, the desert landscapes, maybe even the danger. Each moment we spend here has its own irreducible value. Each act of defiant friendship is self-fulfilling, autotelic. Yesterday we marched in protest in Silwan—some five hundred ordinary Israelis doing the simple, the decent thing—and at first I was wondering where the Palestinians were (most were standing at their windows and doors and watching us), and my colleague Yossi Zeira said to me: "This is *our* task. No one will do it for us. Every good action counts and adds to the pressure. Slowly they will add up and bring change." Alan, walking beside me, said he had felt tired after a day at work and almost didn't come, and then he remembered a phrase from the end of Stephen Poliakoff's film *Glorious 1939*: "It is when the good people, or even those who are only half-good, remain silent that evil flourishes." And there are moments of still deeper insight. When Eileen heard the rhymed slogan we've been chanting—"*Ein kedusha be'ir kvushah,* There Is No Sanctity in an Occupied City"—she said: "Maybe there is sanctity *only* in an occupied city." I think she's right. Nothing in my experience comes as close to the meaning of a word like "holy" as the act of protest against what the municipality and the police are doing in Palestinian East Jerusalem.

That's also what Istvan tells me as we work the buckets by the well. He's a religious man, and to him these Ta'ayush hours in South Hebron are what religion is all about: truth, for example, and loving kindness. "The settlers think that they represent the true Judaism," I say to him, "and sometimes I'm afraid they may be right." "No," he says, "they are certainly wrong." At moments simplicity emerges in the mind, like cleaning a muddy well, and you taste a giddy seriousness, a sudden lightening of the heart.

But some things are simpler than others. Eid has joined us today; we embrace like brothers when I see him. But his life in the village is perhaps no longer viable. People envy him—he is educated, articulate, self-possessed—and some don't like the fact that he has Israeli friends. A few days ago Palestinians came to Umm al-Khair and tried to kill him; he managed to get away. He has a wife and a baby daughter, and it's not clear where he can go; he'd like to study somewhere in Europe. He's good with his hands, artistic by nature. Maybe we'll be able to help him. Then there is Haj Isma'il, with his thirty-three children from four wives. How will he manage to support this huge tribe from his tent in the tiny, precarious *khirbeh* of Bi'r al-'Id?

"So how was jail?" I ask Ezra when he emerges from the well. "*Akhla*—great," he says; "highly recommended." He was imprisoned for a month after Judge Elata Ziskind found him guilty of attacking a police officer during house demolitions at Umm al-Khair. The first week in jail, in Jerusalem, was hard; they refused to allow him to receive books, so he went on hunger strike—for four days he ate nothing, until the prison authorities relented. Afterward he was transferred to Dekel Prison in Beer-Sheva, where things improved. The cell was filthy, he says, and infested with cockroaches who paid no heed to human attempts to drive them away; they slept with him in his bed, emerged from his towel when he showered. One day he asked the commanding officer: "Are these part of the menu or part of the punishment?" He found a fifty-meter stretch of corridor where he was allowed to walk, and every day he would pace it up and down, for hours. He lost a lot of weight. But there's no trace of bitterness in him—quite the contrary, today he seems to me at peace, and full of hope. At lunch I say to him, "I hear you're feeling optimistic." He laughs. "Yes. Just look around. Two years ago we didn't even know the name of this place. These people had been driven off their land, the houses and terraces were destroyed, the wells stopped up. Now we've brought them back and stood by them, and we've helped them to stand up to the settlers and the soldiers and not to be afraid. They are here to stay. They are home. You can train people so they become able to resist. Even a few people like that make a huge difference. In the end we will win. So of course I'm optimistic. You must be optimistic, too, otherwise why would you be here?"

September 25, 2010, An-Nabi Salih

An-Nabi Salih is a hard place. When Ezra heard me say yesterday, in Sheikh Jarrah, that I was going to the village, he said, "Take a helmet. They're violent there, all of them" (he meant: settlers, soldiers, and villagers). Yesterday, at the usual Friday demonstration in the village, the soldiers fired rounds of live ammunition along with rubber-coated bullets and tear gas and stun grenades. I was expecting more of the same today.

The village, north and west of Ramallah, has the great misfortune of having the hard-core settlement of Halamish as its unwanted neighbor. An-Nabi Salih lost some of its lands to the settlement along with access to a freshwater spring, a precious thing in this arid, sun-scorched landscape; the settlers stole the spring, but the villagers were not prepared to surrender it, so there have been many violent clashes, spread over years. The settlers do whatever they can to make the villagers' life miserable, with much success, and the soldiers, as always, back them up.

Today is International Peace Day, and the Palestinian Movement of Non-Violent Resistance, run by Ali Abu 'Awad from Beit Ummar (with offices in Bethlehem), has planned a celebration-cum-workday in An-Nabi Salih. Hundreds of Palestinian activists were supposed to arrive from all over the West Bank—but the army has turned all the buses away and closed the roads. We run into the same roadblocks at the main turnoff from Highway 60 heading north through the West Bank. The soldiers laugh at us when we tell them we're going to An-Nabi Salih. No chance, they say, of getting through. But this is the West Bank, and there is always a way, maybe not an easy way, but some back road or goat track or dirt path that will get you where you're going; so we wind our way for close to two hours, through Jiljiliya and other quite lovely villages until we fetch up at Qarawat Bani Zeid, close to our goal. But there is, Ali tells us, another army roadblock at the entrance to the village. The Tel Aviv party tried to get past them by running a few hundred yards over the hills, and several of the activists were caught and arrested. Do we want to attempt the same tactic?

At least some of us may get through, but we hesitate: is it

worth the hassle of the arrests and the violence? On the other
hand, having come so far, how can we simply turn back? Seven
of us are prepared to run the gauntlet. Finally, at high noon,
Ali leads us down into the rocky terraces and olive groves
underneath An-Nabi Salih. Leaping over the rocky ledges, we
descend to a level that is hopefully beyond the soldiers' range
of vision, and for twenty minutes or so we creep stealthily from
tree to tree and rock to rock, in near-total silence, playing hide-
and-seek, outflanking them, crouching, holding our breath,
hoping to emerge far enough past the roadblock to elude cap-
ture. It's very hot, and I'm thirsty and, by the end, physically
depleted; it's been thirty-three years, I calculate, since I last
engaged in such games, in my basic training in the army. So
absorbed am I in the play that I hardly take in the splendor of
the hills rolling dizzily toward the horizon; but at one point
I do see, just above my head, an olive branch laden with green
fruit almost exploding with ripeness. Soon autumn will come,
and the olive harvest; on the way in the minibus, bouncing
over the back roads, there was even a sweet moment of rain,
with the sharp smell, unlike all others, of wet dust settling to
the ground.

There are eleven of us: seven Ta'ayush volunteers, two Palestinian women in modern dress, head covered, from Beit
Ummar, Alison and Ali himself, tall, graceful, careful, pre-
scient. At one point we almost make a bad mistake, start climbing up too soon, too close to the soldiers; but Ali catches this in
time and leads us back down through the trees and brambles.
When we do move up to the road, we find ourselves very much
inside the village, welcomed warmly by two elderly gentlemen,
who come to shake my hand, and then by a bevy of teenagers.
The first thing I see is a huge sign, in Arabic and English: "The
children of this land deserve our struggle and sacrifices for

peace." Fifteen yards down the main street, another one: "We believe in nonviolence, do you? We are making social change, are you?" A few yards further along: "*La salam ma'a wujud al-ihtilal*, "Making peace means ending the Occupation." Biggest of all, draped over the entrance to the town meeting place: "Keeping our political prisoners behind the bars of tyranny and injustice is inexcusable on International Peace Day."

Do *I* believe in nonviolent struggle? Yes, with all my heart. And I see that I'm not alone—indeed, far from it. We sit at first, rehydrating, under the enormous tree in the village square. Our hosts serve us Turkish coffee and mineral water. We make some friends. One of the village elders says to me with irony (remember yesterday's live ammunition): "Welcome to Eden." Actually, though, he just might be right. The heat intensifies. Eventually, inevitably, it is time for the speeches. Popular Arabic music is blaring at deafening volume from the loudspeakers as we take our seats under a wide canvas. It goes on and on, until, mercifully, a young poet takes the microphone and recites a poem. A passage from the Qur'an is sung. The poet introduces the speakers one by one. I'm weary and, at first, a bit bored.

Normally, I have no patience with political speeches in the villages, but today's surprise me, shake me awake: "We are against violence, we condemn it, we want to be free, the Occupation with its hatred is destroying hope, but we persevere for the sake of our children, and we will win." More poems, dramatically sung or recited, punctuate these orations. Now Ali rises to speak—in English, so that all the Israelis and the foreign volunteers can understand: "I bow my head to all the volunteers who came to An-Nabi Salih today, who struggled past the soldiers and the roadblocks and didn't turn back. Our struggle is complicated and hard, a struggle that we all share—

local leaders of the villages, women, children, families—the first large-scale Palestinian nonviolent movement on the ground, aimed at building a just peace with Israel. When I see Israeli activists coming here to the village, my heart cries with happiness; I am honored to have these people with us. To all the Jews I say: you are not my enemy. The Occupation is your enemy, as it is ours. The Israeli state is a state that eats its children by sending them with weapons to kill and be killed. When you hurt us to the point where we lose our fear of dying, all of us together lose our love of living. They closed off An-Nabi Salih today to keep us out; they know how to put up checkpoints, but they do not know how to fight the feeling of freedom we hold in our hearts. We say to you today, on the Day of Peace: *Peace itself is the way to peace, and there is no peace without freedom.* I am proud to be in An-Nabi Salih, and I promise you: we're gonna make it."

As if on cue, soldiers roll into the village in their jeeps; they do what soldiers do, that is, they threaten, they bully, they make arrests, they take their hostages to an olive grove on the other side of the houses, facing Halamish. Our hosts ask us if we would be prepared to take water to the new arrestees (they don't want to approach the soldiers themselves), so of course we set off through the village streets and down the hill until we find them. Some ten to fifteen soldiers, weighed down by what looks like tons of equipment, green camouflage netting on their helmets and rifles in their arms, are guarding a group of twenty-some students from Birzeit University who came to join today's festivities. We bring water, we chat with the captives, and suddenly it transpires that we've been added to their number; the soldiers won't allow us back into the village. They don't want outsiders in there, they're glad they've thinned the ranks. (The presence of foreigners, especially Israelis, makes it harder for them to shoot.) After a few minutes we tire of this and strike out uphill, dodging the soldiers, who are clumsy, weighed down by their guns and all the rest, as they join hands to create a wall and hold us back, and skirmishes develop, and then the first stun grenade, and it ends with four activists, including Sahar and Lihi, caught, handcuffed and forced to the ground. I am too quick for them, as often, and escape their clutches by following Jonathan farther into the trees.

By the time I regain the village, the main procession—the ritual dénouement of the day—is already forming. I hear mothers telling their young boys to go home, to stay out of it, watch them pushing them away. Originally the idea was to reach the stolen spring, but the soldiers, waiting for us in force at the turn in the road, put an end to this dream. Tear-gas canisters and cartridges of rubber-coated bullets are loaded on to the rifles pointed at the crowd of women, children, men, young and old, many carrying in their arms green saplings that we wanted to plant around the spring. We sit on the pavement with the soldiers almost close enough to touch, they're aiming at us, and I'm a little afraid they might open fire like yesterday, and even more afraid that one of the kids will throw a rock and all hell will break loose, but there's also suddenly no end to the happiness that is washing over me as the light softens to a golden glow and a blessed wind gusts through the trees. People are singing: freedom songs. They swell to a sweet and strident chorus.

March 5, 2011, al-Tawamin

End of winter, early spring: the hills of South Hebron are a shocking green. It won't last long. Very soon now, unless there's one last burst of rain, green will revert to the usual palette of yellow and brown. Already the sun is strong, a taste of the fierce summer to come. The rocky trails are white with asphodels in full bloom—what the Palestinians call *ghosalan* and the Jews call *irit*. On the drive down we pass dozens of almond trees, another white miracle, in their short spring flowering. I am so glad to be back, to be outside in the air and light and not at my desk, to be with these people again, to act.

We work our way slowly uphill over the rocks, a long early-morning walk. We pass a herd of sheep and goats, with their lone Palestinian shepherd; here, on the lower slopes, things are still calm. But on the crest of the hill, where two more herds are grazing happily, a bearded settler, his tzitzit tassles waving frantically as he moves, is already waiting for us. He's there to make trouble, no doubt about that. Although it is Shabbat, he's speaking earnestly into his cell phone, no doubt summoning the soldiers to drive us, and of course the shepherds, off the hill.

And indeed the soldiers rapidly appear, a large unit. The standard ritual commences. "This hilltop is Jewish," the senior commander, a major from the Civil Administration, grimly announces. "Tell your Palestinian friends to leave." He's not overtly mean, in fact by army standards he's almost pleasant, but he's very eager to get us off the grazing grounds. Trouble is, we're quite a large group today, some twenty-five or so, young and old, women and men, a motley crowd of stubborn individualists, not easily pushed around, and we've fanned out over the slopes so he can't just round us up and deliver his orders. He threatens us, as usual: if we don't leave, he'll declare the whole ridge a Closed Military Zone, and then, if we stay, we'll be breaking the law and subject to arrest. Actually, he explains, the Palestinians have already broken the law just by being there, on Jewish soil.

"Jewish soil?" Danny says to him, outraged. "What Jews are you talking about? I'm Jewish, you're Jewish, but we don't own this hill and you have no right to speak in my name. And you know as well as I do that these are the grazing grounds for Palestinian shepherds; we're standing on privately owned Palestinian land." "No," says the major, "the Zionist Federation has taken it over for the settlers who live in Susya" (just a kilometer or so away). "So you're here," I say, "to help the settlers steal this piece of land." No reply. He rustles his map. He consults with his counterpart, an army captain. They're clearly trying to find some correlation between the unwieldy army map in their hands and the recalcitrant terrain in question. Meanwhile, another settler has turned up, with two furious, menacing dogs. Unlike Settler A, Settler B is, I think, a full-fledged lunatic, wild-eyed and racist, the kind one meets in the South Hebron hills relatively often. He curses us bitterly and he curses the soldiers who, he says, had coordinated their moves with the settlers in the middle of the week (again, standard practice); but now, to his immense dissatisfaction, these same soldiers seem unprepared to use sufficient force against us, the Jewish traitors and, even worse, they are actually paying some attention to "stinking Arabs," that is, the young shepherds surrounded by their sheep.

We know this place well. There are two large wells on the hill—hence its name, al-Tawamin, "the Twins." We also know that these wells belong to the Palestinians; we've come here before to help our friends from Bi'r al-'Id and elsewhere draw water and fill tankers. We mention this to the major and, somewhat surprisingly, he at once agrees that the wells are indeed Palestinian and that Palestinians have the right to take water from them. Good, we say, we want to water the herds now. No, he says, you can't do that. Why is that? Because, although the wells indeed belong to Palestinians, the area surrounding them, including the high ridge and slope where we are standing, are off limits to Palestinians. They could, he says, in theory, draw water from the wells, if they could somehow manage to approach them, but they definitely can't bring their sheep there to drink.

He's a reasonable man, our major. He has his orders. I think even he finds them absurd. Anyway, he has a job to do. Perched somewhere near him and the cohort from the regular army, I hear a soldier report that the police are refusing to come unless violence erupts. This may be good news for us. Meanwhile, the sheep are blithely chewing the thorns and leaves they adore; the hilltop is peppered with seemingly bored and somewhat disoriented soldiers, three or four nonchalant shepherds and small, dispersed clumps of peace activists; and Settler A is losing patience and has started berating us, sneering, ordering us to go away. "You're the one who should go away," we say to him, "you shouldn't be here in the first place, you're no better than a common thief." "Where do you want me to go?" he asks, and I know what comes next, "back to Auschwitz?" "Actually," I say, "I was thinking of Tel Aviv."

Ezra approaches me and says, sotto voce: "We're going to bring the sheep to the well, but someone has to distract the soldiers. Go talk to them." "What about?" I say, reluctant. "Just do it," he says, "I'm asking you." OK, it's my turn. Have to think of something. I approach the portly major and say, gently, "Can I ask you a question?" Something in my tone, it seems, catches his attention, and he nods. I continue: "Doesn't it seem a bit crazy to you that this is a Palestinian well, by your own admission, but that the Palestinians can't use it because you've forbidden them to cross the land around it? What are they supposed to do? Parachute the sheep down from helicopters?" "Crazy?" he says, and for a second I get a glimpse of the real person struggling to get out, "Of course it's crazy. Everything down here is crazy. I'm crazy, you're crazy, whatever we do here is crazy, the settlers are crazy, the Palestinians are crazy, even the sheep and goats are crazy. That is why I stick to my orders. They are clear. If you have a problem with the orders, you can talk to your lawyers and take the matter to court. My job is to keep the peace. I let the people of Bi'r al-'Id come here to draw water, if they coordinate with us, in fact I even provide them with a security escort. All kinds of crazy things happen here. I've seen it all. I've been in the territories for thirteen years. Your coming here today is a provocation that makes everything worse."

"Wait a minute," I say. "You've just threatened to declare this hilltop a Closed Military Zone. Don't you know that's illegal? The Supreme Court has banned this maneuver of declaring a Closed Military Zone if it means keeping Palestinian farmers or shepherds from their fields and grazing grounds. We can show you a copy of the decision right now. And anyway, why are you protecting the thieves and not their victims? You see that settlement over there, Susya? In a few years, maybe sooner, you'll be ordered to evacuate it."

"Maybe I will be, maybe I won't," he says. "If they give me the order, I'll do it. It's not up to you and me to decide, anyway."

"Really?" I say. "So who decides, if not you and me? And what about your conscience?"

"Are you asking me to disobey orders, to refuse to serve?"

"No, I'm not, but I'm curious about the state of your conscience."

"I have my orders."

"Yes, I know."

Amiel is listening, bemused, to this futile conversation. He cites Tennyson, deliberately altering the line: "*Ours not to reason why, / ours but to do and die.*" The major is not amused. He points to his soldiers, not far away. "Look at these young guys," he says to me. "What do you want them to do? Do you have a son who served in the army?"

"All three of them did," I say.

"So think about these boys as if they were your sons. You're confusing them. They're serving the state. If they go raiding some place like Yata, one of these nights, looking for terrorists, they might get shot."

"They wouldn't get shot," I say, relishing the tautology, "if they weren't down here in the first place, where they have no business being."

"Look," he says, "let's face it, you and me are Jews, and my job is to protect Jews."

"No," I say, "that is certainly not your job." Do I have to spell it out? He's an almost honest man. As for the sheep, it appears they drank their fill.

February 23, 2013, Susya, Shamasteh Family Lands, Zanuta

It's cold, blustery, a gray-green day. This is that evanescent moment when the hills turn green, like in Ireland, and the red anemones break through the hard surface of the soil. We're at a bus stop on the highway near Susya, waiting for the Shamasteh family to pick us up. Here's their story. They own a large swath of good land, and they have the registry documents to prove it, but the Susya settlers have stolen a big chunk of these holdings; now the Civil Administration in its wisdom has declared these fields "in dispute," as at Umm al-Ara'is.[16]

Suddenly we see, in the distance, white-clothed settlers herding their sheep right through the Shamasteh fields, with a large posse of soldiers close behind them, and Palestinians gathering in apparent protest. We set off over the hill to join them. Haj Khalil, one of those ageless, wizened farmers, tough, determined, self-sufficient, is planting almond seeds. He has an iron pike that he pounds deep into the earth with a hammer, then rapidly, lovingly, he takes it out and places the almond seed in the hole he has made, and a young boy pours water from a plastic bottle. The soldiers, angry and helpless, are fluttering around him as he strides from one rocky patch to another. In goes the pike, then the embryonic almond, the water, and on to the next. "You can't do this," they are yelling at him, "we're telling you to stop, we'll arrest you, listen to us." He pays no attention whatsoever. Around him hover his sons and grandsons and a few heavyset earth-women, perhaps his wives or daughters-in-law. The eldest son veers unevenly between his father and the soldiers; he shields the old man as best he can even as he tries to placate the soldiers: "I'll tell him, just give me a moment." But no one can keep up with Haj Khalil, and no human act can compare with the stark splendor of defiance. At least twenty new almond trees will surely spring from the pits he manages to open and impregnate before the soldiers finally bring him to a halt or he runs out of seeds.

Impish, satisfied, happy, he seats himself leisurely on the ground and takes out a pipe, which he proceeds to light very slowly, entirely focused on this demanding task. The pipe is man's work, and Haj Khalil is equal to it. He offers me a puff, and I accept, immediately choking on the smoke. He points to the soldiers and says to me, "They have no fear of God, or of Moses, or of Jesus, or of the Prophet. They have no fear of doing wrong." He seems almost to feel sorry for them. You can see why. They're still fussing with their cell phones and their guns and their papers; they're out of their element here. Finally they produce the inevitable order declaring this field, a Shamasteh field, a Closed Military Zone. The order comes with a map. The commanding officer, looking frantically for some useable landmark, points to the dirt footpath where he is standing and says: "You see this line? You cannot cross this line. You can be there, on the other side of the path, but not here, on this side of it. Am I clear? Anyone on this side of the line will be arrested immediately."

Reluctantly, the Palestinians—by now a sizable mass of men, women, children—move to the edge of the footpath. What else can they do? But the officer is now pleased with himself and with the arbitrary line he has drawn in the desert. He smiles, relieved. "Excellent," he says, "everyone is in his place, and everything is in order." That's his job in life, in this best of all possible worlds. He makes order.

He's not a bad man, by the way. Just happens to be a thief.

The women set about making fire inside a small rectangular stone pen a few meters down the hillside. Soon there is tea. They form a semicircle outside the pen while the ragamuffin kids race over the stones. A picnic: pastoral, natural, simple, except for the uninvited guests. Against the grand sweep of the hills you can see sheep, the sharp glow of the fire, the blue-red-black of the womens' dresses, the roughness of rock; behind us, guns and more guns. One of the women decides it's time to give the soldiers a piece of her mind. "What are you doing here? This is our land. You have no right to be standing here. It's forbidden. It's wrong, *haram*. You come here every day with your lies and your guns. You drive us away. Who do you think you are? God will punish you."

Ella overhears the soldiers planning, on their radiophones,

to demolish the stone pen where the Palestinian women have just made fire. They'll wait till we're gone, of course. Then, with nobody watching and no one to protest, they'll destroy another small sign of the owners' presence on this land.

These farmers and their wives need to tell the story, so I hear how one day some years back they came here to plow only to find that the fields had been sown the day before by settlers. Since then they're in the courts. One of the men from the Batsh clan—a subdivision of Shamasteh—traces the tortured history for me. Their name, Batsh, he says, is mentioned in the Qur'an. Haj Khalil is still peacefully savoring his pipe.

But farther up the hill there is trouble. Another party of soldiers has chosen a sacrificial victim. They're threatening to arrest one of the young men, for no evident reason. They've copied down the number of his identity card and phoned it in to whoever is manning the computer at headquarters. We rush up to film this, to try to intervene. The soldiers have surrounded their prey, who appears resigned. Suddenly his formidable mother appears. "Musa," she calls, "come with me. Now." He gives her a look that suggests there's not much he can do. She, however, can't be stopped. You won't believe it, but she literally pounces on her son, enfolds him in her capacious arms, in her loose black dress, and prods and pushes him past the soldiers in the direction of freedom. They hurl themselves against her, but she remains uncowed. In a wild, relentless choreography, she snatches him from their hands, not once but five, six times, each time maneuvering him downward and away, beyond their grasp, as she cries out at them in continuous derision, a steady flow of thick invective that seems to leave them stunned and impotent. Finally, he's gone, slipped away. They send him a message with his father: next time they'll get him.

So that's what a mother is for.

She, and Haj Khalil, are my teachers today.

Ezra was in court again this week for what he calls the "case of the dogs" as opposed to the "war-crimes' case." Some time ago he insulted a high-ranking officer of the Civil Administration. The officer told him he was leaving his post in the territories. Ezra quoted an Arabic proverb: "One dog goes and another dog comes." The officer sued him. The judge, either bored or bemused by this case, said: "At least it's better than the last time." The last time was when Ezra rightly accused some other officer of war crimes. He hates all generals with a passion. Many times in the field, I've tried, usually unsuccessfully, to get him to hold his tongue. The verdict will be rendered in about two weeks.

June 29, 2013, Umm al-'Amad

Ahmad likes to sing. Almost from the moment we turn up—around 7:00 a.m., when it's still deliciously cool with light wind and cloud—he's been singing happily as he keeps an eye on his goats. Ahmad is something between a boy and a young man. Seems happy. So do the goats, feasting without pause on the varied menu of thorns that this hill offers them. The songs, too, are varied. They include the latest hit in Palestine, the song a young singer from Gaza, Muhammad 'Assaf, sang to win the Arab Idol competition last week.

Mostly Ahmad sings songs of love and yearning. A Palestinian idyll: the shepherd out on the hills with his flock. And the hills are ravishing this morning, the contours sharply etched, tinged with blue. In the distance the village of Karma spills over the rocks. Umm al-'Amad, where Ahmad lives, is hidden by the slope and the olive trees.

There's a stain on the idyll. Needless to say, we're not alone. Two jeeps of soldiers from the Lavi regiment — regular army — are here to watch. Their lieutenant is a burly Druze. Heavily armed, they station themselves on the dirt path that they have declared to be the boundary that Palestinians cannot traverse. With them is the security officer, also armed, of the large settlement of Otniel, which sits on lands stolen from Umm al-'Amad and other villages nearby.

For some reason today, unlike other times at Umm al-'Amad, everything proceeds peacefully. For once the soldiers make no attempt to interfere with the grazing, and the shepherds carefully keep away from the entirely arbitrary boundary. Ahmad sings his songs. We chat and joke and laugh; the goats munch thorns. Slowly the sun warms to its summery task.

A couple of hours go by. I decide it's going to be an easy, even boring day.

I don't hear the words. Only later I'm told that Ahmad, talking with the officer, asked the latter if he fasts on Ramadan. (The fast begins in ten days' time.) The answer was no. Ahmad said that means the Druze will burn in Hell. But maybe it wasn't quite like this; I can't say. In any case, I suddenly see the officer dragging Ahmad onto the forbidden boundary path and then arresting him. He pushes him, surrounded by soldiers, into one of the jeeps. By now we're milling around, stunned, on the path. I'm tempted to throw myself down in front of the jeep. But I'm unsure of what's happened, and why. The jeep takes off with its prisoner.

Now what? We're angry. We weren't prepared for the sudden transition from halcyon morning to the dark poison of the Occupation. Bitterly, we speak our minds. "What do you think you're doing? Why did you arrest him? Why are you being so childish? Some hero you are, lording it over children. This is how you choose to show off your power?" The officer says that Ahmad stepped onto the path and was therefore arrested. But we saw him dragging him onto the path himself, and we've filmed this. Scornfully, we tell him so, over and over. He doesn't answer. His face is already set in stone. He's feeling insulted, no doubt about that, and Ahmad's crime, it appears, was just this—"insulting a public servant." It's a punishable legal offense, although the court, if it goes that far, may not be overly impressed. In any case Ahmad is to be handed over to the police, whom the lieutenant has summoned on his phone. It's also possible that the officer was simply waiting for an opportunity to flex his muscles and make an arrest; maybe he was irritated by the patriotic song of Muhammad 'Assaf that Ahmad was singing. Who can say?

Time, which had been rippling along smoothly, slows down. There is palpable pain in the air, in me. Suddenly I notice that it's hot and dry—summer in the desert. The officer is impassive, immovable. His body language speaks of supercilious defense, as if he were standing, uncaring, in a concrete bunker. He has the power to dispose of his victim however he wants. We hurl our futile arguments at him and his soldiers. No reply. I have no words, but I let my eyes lock onto his, and for a very long moment we stare at one another, under the sun, in wordless communication. I feel enraged. I am looking at the naked arbitrariness of power as it targets the most accessible, usually the weakest, victim. I am looking into the face of the Occupation.

Long minutes pass. He stands at the edge of the field, his soldiers lined up on either side. There's no way to reach him, to reason or persuade. There's nothing more to do. The orphaned goats, by now satiated, are huddled together in conference, peacefully chewing their cud.

What will happen to Ahmad? Probably nothing awful. He'll be hauled off to the police station at Kiryat Arba, kept waiting there for hours, perhaps overnight, handcuffed, interrogated, fingerprinted, photographed. It will be a bit scary: he'll be alone amid the men with guns. Eventually, in all likelihood, they'll let him go on payment of a deposit, something between five hundred and two thousand shekels—a very large sum for an impoverished family of shepherds, and one which can almost never be retrieved even after the case is settled. Then he'll come home. It's also always possible that the case will ramify unexpectedly, that they'll concoct some other charge, that things will drag on indefinitely. No Palestinian can hope for justice at the hands of the Occupation police, or the military courts.

Still, it's a small incident, no need to exaggerate. They'll probably let him go. And yet—sometimes it's the small things that most starkly show the truth.

Now, in the distance, the figure of a woman appears. She is struggling uphill in the fierce heat along the dirt path. She's clearly agitated. She wears a black scarf on her head, a rather lovely patterned dress of magenta checks and rhomboids. She's Ahmad's mother, and she's heard the news.

There's no limit to her fury. We try to explain to her what's happened, but she has no patience for our words. Very rapidly she locates the officer and unleashes her tongue. "*Haram 'aleyk*, shame on you. You should be ashamed of yourself. Who do you think you are? Allah sees everything. Allah is stronger than you. He'll punish you. May He do to your children what you have done to my son. Shame on you! What did he do? He got up in the morning, he didn't even have a drink of water, he ate no breakfast, he came out here on his own land with his goats and sheep, and now you're taking him away. When you looked at him did you see some *ra'is*, some politician or prime minister, some big man? He's just a boy, a shepherd. You've burned my heart. You're a big hero, swaggering over children, over women. You're weak, concerned only with your self-importance, your *sharaf*. Nothing else interests you. You know nothing of justice, of what is right. But we're not afraid of you. I'm staying here, I'm not going anywhere until you give me back my son. You can kill me if you like, it would be better." She raises her arms to the skies, she invokes the name of Allah, she turns this way and that, swirling, raging, bitter with scorn. From time to time she lays her hand on her heart.

It's a performance like no other. A torrent of juicy Arabic washes over the rocks and thorns. Inventive, fearless, she curses him and the soldiers for the misery they've caused. We support her as best we can, we address the officer again. "All this because you've been offended? Look what you've done to this mother." Frozen, unyielding, he suddenly blurts out, "I'm not offended, *lo pagua*." He's trying to say, it seems, that Ahmad committed a serious offense, something beyond the personal, but Amiel immediately sees the meaning of what he's just uttered: "If you're not offended, then there's no basis for the arrest; the boy insulted nobody. Let him go." The lieutenant lapses back into stony, sullen silence. No contact. The mother sits down on a stone, still crying out her refrain: "*Haram 'aleyk, haram 'aleykum*, Shame, Shame!" She demands to know what her son did wrong; the lieutenant won't say. "He didn't do anything," says another of the shepherds, trying to comfort.

One of the soldiers emerges from the jeep with a thick bunch of green grapes. He offers them to his comrades, who seem entirely indifferent to the drama unfolding before them. Noisily, hungry, he gulps down the grapes. The officer stirs, stone momentarily reverting to flesh: "Don't eat in front of them," he says. But the mother has seen them: "You eat and drink and have a fine time, and *he* didn't even have a glass of water today."

It's a miniature of the Occupation. As Yigal says, "First they steal the land and expel you, then, when you complain, they feel entitled to feel insulted and arrest you." I've been through many moments far worse than this, more consequential and devastating; but the mother's agony is of a different order.

All this time I am reduced to muteness. I keep trying to imagine what we might say that could turn things around. Can't find the words. Numb in mind. I can see that the officer is in a zone of sheer, cussed pique, unable to budge, unable to lose face before his men. He seems to me trapped in a situation he himself created, heavy with ego. I don't think I can reach him. I can't believe he is unmoved, on some level, by the mother's distress, but I can see that he's unable to address it, or to act.

"If only there were something useful to say," I mumble to Soryl, a friend from Montreal. To my surprise—the first of several in store for me—she takes this statement seriously and urges me: "Go talk to him."

"I don't know what to say, I don't think I can get through to him."

"What's there to lose?"

OK, maybe she's right. It's worth a try. Not that I have any hope. I'm sure he'll reject anything I say out of hand. And I have no idea how to begin. Anyway, I pick my way over the rocks to the edge of the dirt path. Where'd he go? Must be here somewhere. I look on the lee side of the jeep. Sure enough, he's there, alone, talking on his cell phone—probably trying to get the police to hurry up. Maybe on some unconscious level I register that he's out of his men's sight, and thus this moment could be opportune. I'm not thinking clearly, in fact not thinking at all. I approach him, he turns toward me. "Can I talk to you?" I say, no sting attached.

"Yes." Another surprise.

I introduce myself. I tell him I'm from the university. "Look,"

I say, "I see that some situation has developed here, wouldn't you like to bring it to an end?"

"Yes. But I can't do anything when people are screaming at me and there's chaos, *fauda, balagan.*"

"Wait a minute," I say, waking up, "You mean if I get them to stop screaming and we calm things down, you'll release him?"

"Maybe."

I go back to my friends to report. We back off. An infinitesimal shift. There's a question of whether we can ask the mother to quiet down for a second. No: can't do it. She has to have the freedom to speak her heart. At least that. But now another figure is making his way uphill through the dust. Ahmad's father—balding, tall, dignified, in an ironed blue shirt—arrives on the scene.

He speaks firmly and gently, mostly in Hebrew; from where we're standing, we can barely hear the words. "If you were insulted by something my son said, then I, too, am insulted by it." It's exactly the right tone. The shift is more than infinitesimal now. Over the next minutes, a solution is achieved. They'll bring Ahmad back and file no charges. The father will explain to him, clearly and sternly, how to comport himself vis-à-vis the soldiers. That's the condition. The Druze soldier will listen to this paternal lesson, father to son. They call the mother over, and she understands; the curses stop.

The officer seeks me out to tell me. Apparently, he has a need to explain himself. "I'm here," he says, "to guard over everyone—these people, and the settlers on top of the hill, and you, too. That's my job. We're letting him go." I nod, relieved. The job description is revealing, though unpersuasive. I can't quite bring myself to thank him—I'm all too aware of the mess he's made—but slowly and carefully I say, "That's good." I'm sorry, now, as I write, that I couldn't find in myself the generosity to thank him after all. I think that for a short moment he overcame something in his nature.

He asks if I'm with one of the organizations. "Ta'ayush," I proudly say; "from almost the beginning, years ago." I think I see him wince. He asks me what I teach at the university, and I tell him. He seems curious and slightly amused. "When you finish with all this," I say, "you can come learn some Indian language with us." He smiles. "Not me. I'm staying here. I like the army."

One of the jeeps turns around and drives off; ten minutes later they're back with Ahmad. High noon. In the white dust of South Hebron, the parents embrace their son. At once sheepish and insouciant, his wrists still bearing the deep marks of the cuffs, he goes off with his shepherd friends. In silence we walk the parents home.

6

TRUTH, TRUST, CONSCIENCE

1.

I'm a person mostly without faith. Long ago a close friend, a rabbi, Jim Ponet, said to me: "If you have to believe in something, it means you think it's not true."[17] So I can't say I believe in God, though I sometimes think he's with us in critical moments in the hills, and I've also seen him or her, with my own eyes, many times in India. I have a particular fondness for the intimate, unforgettable Jewish god of my childhood; I thought then, I still think, that he must be lonely and often sad, like me.

There are, despite everything, some sentences I would like to believe in. Marcus Aurelius—perhaps my best friend in these expeditions into Palestine—says: "Has someone wronged you? He wrongs himself" (4.26). If only this were true. Here I enter a space of wonder. Maybe it is true. Maybe all of us know that it's true, so that it's not something we have to believe in. Marcus has this overpowering faith in the goodness of the natural cosmos, and the sentence in question follows necessarily from that faith. At the same time, it is profoundly linked to a notion of one's own inner freedom to act-through-thinking. The sentence directly preceding the one just quoted is: *haploson sea-ton,* "Uncomplicate yourself."[18] As if this business of simplifying one's consciousness were within our power, though nearly all my experience of myself over nearly seven decades suggests that I will never be simple. For that very reason, I want to put this sentence, *haploson seaton,* on the door to my office at the university.

Yet at times there is a real-life simplicity about South Hebron. Often it's like a litmus test: you can see in broad daylight who the thief is and who the innocent victim. So out of a starting state rife with doubt, without saints or heroes, with the surreal confabulation of conflicting human wishes, fears, agonies, swirling around us, we gather ourselves up to do what is, evidently, simply, the right thing. Not always, but often, it is quite easy to know what the right thing is, under the circumstances.

We, in Ta'ayush, and maybe all people, act out of choice, though, as I've said, not everyone knows there is choice. Marcus thought so, too: "Do not hold to the opinions of him (or her) who decides to act in violence and who wants you to decide to do the same" (4.11). And then the inevitable conclusion derived from the recommendation just cited: "See things as they truly are." Truly—*kat' aletheian.* There is such a thing as truth, as true perception, and such a perception will hopefully keep you from thinking what your violent rival thinks and from doing what he does. Thinking freely divides us starkly, probably irrevocably, from the thoughts and deeds of those who do wrong.

I suppose I believe this to be true. Note the subjunctive. You can see why Marcus is such a good friend. I almost hear him whispering in my ear at moments when the soldiers are inflicting pain, or when they are about to arrest some of us, or when they trot out the soggy bits of thought that they've been taught to believe in instead of thinking for themselves. It is in the nature of a soldier to surrender not only his life, his future, his self, but — first and foremost — his mind. That is what everything in his training aims at achieving. Very few manage to resist this process. Those who do, have the extraordinary character of the ordinary decent human being.

Can truth, then, ever be simply, undeniably true? Can it be true in a singular way, not in the multiplicity of viewpoints and possible truths that comprise the web of everyday existence? Is it, for example, true that the Occupation is wicked at the root and cannot be justified by any rational means? Yes. It is true.

How do I know that it is true? I'm not the one to offer an answer to a question that has exercised philosophers ever since philosophers have existed. There are criteria of knowing that many have put forward and that one might embrace ad hoc, when the circumstances are right and these criteria appear to suit our experience. It is even possible — of this I am sure — to teach people to be rational, or more rational, through patient Socratic examination of how thought happens and how it works. It is one of life's sad pleasures to be trained to a deeper rationality.

But as it happens, long experience in South Hebron also teaches you something about seeing, or not seeing, what is truly there. I want to probe this notion in the light of my memories, without making all-embracing claims. "Truth" is a dense, thick word. There are forms of truth that are not relevant to this discussion — factual truth, for example, which generally tends to the disastrous. It is true that we age, get sick, and die, suffering great losses along the way. Even if we know that facts are "made," *facta*, and not simply given with the world, it is not that kind of truth that concerns us at this moment.

Let us look, once more, at ethical truths that impinge upon our very being and that require, minimally, true perception. I am not speaking of the truth of mathematics or of physics, the movement of planets and stars and molecules. Such truths are also problematic, but they do not impinge on this discussion— although there are moments, when night falls and we are still in the field, that looking up at the stars may bring temporary relief from rage or pain.

Truth, I have said, can be very simple. We are driving along and suddenly we see, close to the road, an elderly Palestinian shepherd sitting on a stone with his head in his hands while settler toughs mock him, torment him, strike at him. All around him stand his baffled, orphaned sheep. We stop, of course, we rush to his aid. The settlers now turn against us. One of them, a young man, or maybe more boy than man, says to me, "I know why you're here. You hate me." I say to him, "Actually, you're wrong. I hate what you're doing right now, but I don't hate you. Believe it or not, I may even love you." He fizzles out like a balloon. But he is still very angry, and after a moment's thought he says to me, "You're a Jew, so I am not allowed to hate you, according to the Torah. But if I could, I would certainly hate you." Hatred rings true. What we saw happening also left no room for doubt.

If causing great harm to innocent beings is morally, humanly, unacceptable, then a system like that of the Occupation that is entirely rooted in such acts of inflicting pain must be wicked, and the sorts of things that settlers say about it must be wrong—that God gave the Jews, and only the Jews, the land of Israel, for example, and even commanded them to hold on to it at all cost, or to wrest it by force from the hands of any rival claimants; or that by "redeeming" the land in this way, the Jews will hasten the arrival of the Messiah. As I write these last clauses, their patent foolishness embarrasses me; I almost erased them out of shame. It is even hard to believe that Jewish people, of all the peoples in the world, can believe them. There it is again, that impoverished quality of belief. I grew up in a world, and in a family, where Jewish people had far better things to believe in.

Motivation matters when it comes to establishing criteria for ethical truth. Suppose a truth claim is clearly driven by greed, or by hate, or by racism, or by smugness and arrogance. In theory, these affective components of the claim might not matter. Either X is true or it is not true. But such a theory can't be adequate when it comes to establishing ethical truth. The emotions that precede the claim and that are called upon to justify it can also falsify it, as we know well from everyday living.

In fact, truth itself may be more of a feeling than an act of thinking. I have said that South Hebron supplies a litmus test for values, and thus for truthfulness. How does the test work in practice? Most often, one knows in a bodily way. If your mind is at least a little free, you will know from the pores of your skin, or a powerful burst of feeling in your stomach or chest, or from your fingertips and toenails, what the right thing is to do. You don't have to believe in anything for that knowledge to emerge inside you. By the same token, your bones and tissues will usually tell you if you do wrong, though you may not pay attention.

We, the activists, all know this from long experience. I asked my friend Guy Hircefeld how he came to Taʿayush. He spoke of truth and the real: "Taʿayush is the most real thing there is. We speak only the truth, with no facade, no cover-up. We tell it as it is, no apologies." That kind of knowledge precipitates action. "The more poisoned the public space is—by the government and the general public—the stronger I feel the need to act."

A faithless person like me needs a body to know what is true and what is right. I stand before an officer of the Civil Administration, who has just announced to us that the 'Awad family cannot plow the lands that the district court has, after a long legal battle, recognized as theirs. Or rather, the officer has taken us for a long hike over the hills to show them where he will allow them to plow: Not here near the well; not here, too close to the settlement; not on the southern slope, or the northern slope, or the eastern slope, or the western slope; not in the wadi, and not in the plots adjacent to the wadi—but yes, here, you see this little square patch of stubble by the main road? Here you can plow, *tafaddalu*, "be my guests." He's an affable, friendly person, this officer, but look what he's just done. I feel my heart kicking into protest; I feel nausea in the pit of my stomach. I know wickedness when I see it, as it truly is: *kat' aletheian*, the Aurelian phrase.

There are some other, dependable signs of truth of the type we are contemplating. Although weighty and consequential, it has a light and airy gravitas. It takes life as it comes, without imparting further grimness. It is the enemy of all that is earnest. It is deliciously unsentimental and unselfconscious. No false heroics, no utopian romance—although it does carry a whiff of eros, like most good things. It feels real. It creates both breath and room to breathe.

Such expansiveness is intrinsic to true perception. A broader vision overrules a constricted one. Similarly, what expands my own self, and my awareness, has a natural relation to truth. An existential truthfulness would then be linked to what makes me more, rather than less, alive. A moral act that emerges out of true perception and that for that reason deepens awareness of my friend's pain—possibly also of my enemy's pain, no less than of my own—will set me free. Awareness like this dwells in my body, in my very breath, and speaks to me from dark and hidden places inside, where truth abides.

Recently, an unusual case came to light in Israel of a man named Alon Mizrachi, who was a dyed-in-the-wool right-wing fanatic, filled with hatred for Palestinians and for people like me, but who, under special circumstances, turned himself around and joined the peace camp. He has said about himself, about how he lived before the change he underwent: "You have to extinguish something big in yourself" [*tzarich lechabot mashehu gadol be-tochecha*]. Listen to how he said it, in the active voice: You have to turn yourself off. It's a high price to pay for transient sadistic pleasures, for indulging one's hate.

One pays for cruelty in the currency of aliveness. From what I have seen in the field, I conclude that my wishful thought from before must be true—that one cannot hurt another without killing something or someone in oneself.

2.

There are other ways to address this problem. One could, for instance, start by weeding away what must clearly be false, a form of lying. It's not so hard to do that. Minor, almost trivial examples crop up day by day (but what is trivial in this struggle?). In June 2016, the President of Ben-Gurion University in the Negev, Rivka Carmi, canceled the award of the Berelson Prize by the Department of Political Science in her university to the peace organization Breaking the Silence. Professor Carmi justified her act by saying that Breaking the Silence is "not within the consensus." She's right about that.

"Within the consensus" is the last place I, or any thinking person, would want to be. It is astonishingly easy to compromise one's soul. Remember Marcus: "Do not hold to the opinions of him (or her) who decides to act in violence and who wants you to decide to do the same." Henry David Thoreau said it well, at the same time supplying us with another valuable, eminently practical criterion for identifying truth:

"The greater part of what my neighbors call good I believe in my soul to be bad, and if I repent of anything, it is very likely to be my good behavior. What demon possessed me that I behaved so well?"

The consensus is always what one's neighbors call good. If you find yourself inside it, you're very likely to be in the wrong, as you are if you obey the laws of a wicked system. Like Aurelius, Thoreau thought that truth and goodness are near synonyms—that what is good must also be true, and vice versa—and he added another two adjectives that might fit the landscapes of South Hebron: "All good things are wild and free." I'd like to think that this is right, romantic as it sounds.

3.

But we can go further toward tracing the contours—at least the contours—of ethical truth; further than the possibly reliable but nonetheless impressionistic criteria I have suggested. "Weeding away the false" is a matter of judgment often made crystal clear in the field. I know for certain, without need for further examination, that nearly everything the soldiers tell us there, and most of what the violent settlers we encounter say to us, or rather scream at us, is in the category of lying—because it falls under the rubric of coercive and instrumental use of human beings, the first and most fundamental human sin, infinitely worse than eating of the fruit of that well-known tree. (Was that really a sin? Had Adam not tasted the fruit, I could not be writing these pages.) Using people instrumentally, for one's own egoistic goals or those of one's tribe, inevitably entails inflicting pain. Anyone who lends a hand to that is remote from truth. Any god who appears to demand that is a false god. This is not a subjective criterion.

Truth—moral or existential truth—is, however, a still more expansive business than this singular criterion implies. There will always be cases of inherent ambiguity, where the question of instrumentality alone will not suffice to define the true or, for that matter, the real. These are the interesting cases. Here our experience in the South Hebron hills has added value. I have said that most of our moral judgments, and not only in Palestine, take place under conditions of profound uncertainty. However clear-cut the litmus test, the frame in which it is embedded is certain to be more complex. In a situation of tribal war, like in Israel-Palestine, no side can have a monopoly over truth.

But moral truth is unlikely to be a matter of minute calculation. It involves knowledge of a different order. Here we will have to invoke a notion of conscience and its relation to the self. Surprisingly, it's not at all clear that we need the latter in order to have the former. Probably because of my professional formation—the kinds of things I read every day—but not only for that reason, I am somewhat partial to the Buddhist notion that there is no self-thing, no object that could be given the name of "self." Yet almost at every step I take in those hills, I am deeply aware of myself as a stubbornly personal being of varying degrees of aliveness. I can also tell, usually without much thought, if I slip into a mode of self-betrayal, a false self that might be tempted to comply with what some fool of an officer is ordering me to do, for example. And there are moments of dullness of mind or heart and numbness of soul, to use another rather spooky word.

All right, let us look for another word, hopefully one not starkly delineated. I could be happy with the Greek *psyche* as it evolved from Homer to Plato, though not in the sense of a dualistic fissure within the human person—not, that is, as some metaphysical piece of myself that is distinct from the physical, bodily pieces. The *psyche* thinks, feels, knows, and dreams. Whether it ever dies or not is something I can't know or say. We have a somewhat parallel Indian notion of the *jivatman*, the part of the person that is alive, though not as alive as a nonpersonal dimension of wholeness that is usually called the *atman*, "self," plain and simple. Well, actually not so simple. Whether there is a real self or not, false selves certainly exist. We all have them. To see through them, to see what is really there, one needs a conscience, and fortunately, each of us has been provided with one, or at least a potential for one, though we may not use it very often. My friend Yaron Ezrahi likes to say that a clean conscience is one that has not been used.

Here is what Vladimir Jankélévitch has to say about that: "The moral conscience is not a particular thing in the mind like the color blue, the association of ideas, or the love of women. The moral conscience does not *exist*. But we discover our conscience proper on the day when certain actions that are legal or indifferent or permitted by the police inspire in us an insuperable disgust."[19] Thus conscience, apparently, not unlike the Buddhist nonself, is mostly a potential capable of being activated, if we are lucky, under special, or maybe even ordinary, conditions—thus capable of becoming real. Bodily sensation is a good indicator of whether this conscience-part of ourselves has been turned on or not. Disgust at what one sees is, I think, only one such indicator. My moral conscience, such as it is, seems to inhabit the surface of my skin and to inform my ability to love. It comes from a site where the word "moral" has not yet been born, and only from that dark place does it reach toward my mind.

It comes not with faith but with trust. I know I can trust what I am feeling when I see gratuitous cruelty enacted. But can two conflicting, opposite acts of cruelty, by Y to Z and by Z to Y, cancel each other out? Can I inflict cruelty on another person in order to avoid hurting myself? The more enlightened among the settlers sometimes resort to this argument. They claim that to surrender what is theirs, or (even worse) ours, in order to avoid hurting Palestinians who happen to be there in place, violates elementary morality. It's a very old, unhappy, worn-out Zionist argument. The settlers are wrong about that—their claim on the lands in question is pale, "mythical" in the bad sense of the word, and thus, in my view, far weaker than Palestinian claims—but one sees how quickly doubt percolates upward when conscience is activated or invoked.

Such doubts can be put to rest, at least sometimes, by clear thinking, or by thinking things through. But we may have discovered something of interest. Unlike freedom, that is, the true inner freedom with which we are innately endowed and which is indubitable by virtue of our experience, ethical truth is often a *dubitable* truth. It demands depth and breadth as we try to think it through, and it can easily subvert its initial premises. Ethical truth can no doubt be differentiated from lies, if we feel our way along, but such truth does not cover the whole field of its purported application. More simply stated, this kind of truth is always wider than the way we state it or think it. It emerges from a state of potential fullness and is far fuller than what we make of it. It is that fullness that we experience, in some measure, when we allow ourselves to see things as they are, *kat' aletheian.*

I'm afraid this means that the so-called correspondence theory of truth, so often linked to Kant, has to be set aside.

Ethical and existential truths do not correspond to the objects of our cognition. They exceed our cognition by far. Their plenitude, which we know from experience, is like the elusive plenitude of the dream, which we also, however, perhaps despite ourselves, cannot but recognize as true. Fullness is of the order of expansion—a horizon extending beyond its visible limits. Out of that fullness, often ambiguous and unthinkable, we must act.

Spinoza defined pleasure, or happiness, as the transition from a state of lesser perfection to a state of greater perfection.[20] I think that truth must be like that—a transition, a broadening of perception, a deepening of who and what we are. Moral truth is a passionate and, in my experience, an active way of being and feeling. Without whole-hearted passion, we cannot recognize it as ours. Moreover, the expansiveness of truth must imply that truth is in continuous movement, resistant to fixation, stable contours, or longevity, also immune to anything that smacks of an absolute. The search for dependable contours—an enduring and stable theology or epistemology—is the search for a false god. Similarly with seeing things as they are: for are they not always in movement? It is only as they move that we can see them at all. An existential ethics cannot be at rest.

4.

Before I conclude this meditation, I need to say something more obviously rooted in the concrete and the visible. I want to speak of the landscapes of the South Hebron hills and their link to truth. Even after all these years, I find it hard to contain the juxtaposition of malice and overpowering natural beauty. It feels wrong. Wickedness does not belong in these landscapes.

I understand, I know from inside, the particular sadness that inheres in beauty. The problem with beauty, said Hans Sachs, is not to understand it but to bear it. That, however, is very different from bearing the presence of wickedness in the wide vistas of these hills.

For a few short weeks in spring, the anemones push through the rocky soil amid sudden bursts of green. The green does something to your eyes. I blink in unbelief. Then it's gone, and summer happens, a burning white heat all day long until, in late afternoon, the hills turn mauve and blue for an hour before dark.

Goats trickling over the hills amid the rocks and thorns, white doves in their skyward spiral, white clouds over the open desert. Wind, the cutting edge of silence. Tents, caves, ruins. More goats. I have loved it from the start. I assume that many of my settler foes love it, too, in their own way, though a certain leap of faith is needed if I am to believe this deeply. I'll tell you why. We have seen settlers from Chavat Maon spreading poison in the fields of Palestinian Twaneh. I saw the deer that died from that poison, and the goats who became sick. Can you poison the land you love? Or is that, in some perverse way, our human default? Then there is the sheer ugliness of so many of the settlements. The older ones, by now, have the red tiled roofs and stone facades that are meant to proclaim their permanence. These homes do not slip into the contours of the hills as Palestinian village homes do, but at least they are not as hideous as the drab caravans and spindly water towers and barbed-wire fences of the so-called "illegal outposts" that litter the landscape of South Hebron. It is an everyday experience to watch settlers emerge, with their machine guns, from these miserable barracks, as if deliberately compounding the ugliness. Guns are ugly. I know, I used to carry one, too.

Occasionally I wonder if the settlers really see the landscape in which they have planted themselves. At Carmel many of the newer homes are almost windowless, though the settlement is perched on a hill with a commanding view of the desert and wadis. Why no windows? Do they wish to look only inward, away from the harshness, away from the shadowy figures whose fields they have taken? Yet I have met settlers in South Hebron who seemed to me genuinely, in some sense spiritually, at home in the landscape and in love with it. Some of them are gentle souls who have strayed into a fanatical and lethal vision without meaning to cause hurt. Let us recognize that they, too, can love. Such mutations happen when a person thinks and speaks of an absolute. Often our Palestinian friends tell us that as far as they're concerned, the settlers can stay; there is plenty of room—but only on condition that they act like human beings. Maybe that is what will happen.

But for now, we have a landscape, ravishing beyond words or thought, that is being cruelly violated, torn apart, raped, poisoned, destroyed. It is in the nature of a colonial venture to do that. The true custodians of these hills and terraces and valleys haunt them, still, with their herds and tents. As for the farmers, they have not lost the intimacy of a man or woman with the soil. How many times have I heard them utter the phrases of despair to the soldiers who are driving them off the land: "These are my fields. They need me. I have come to plant, or to harvest, to water, to plow." For them, the land is a living being, in need of nurture. Prevented from offering them this care, the farmer withers in his soul. Perhaps among you who may be reading this page there are some who have seen and known this ache of the farmer for his stolen field—this grief born of a bonding that only human malice can sever.

One should never assume that rocks and trees and thorns

cannot listen or know. There are many degrees and modes of lying, but you cannot deceive a landscape like that in the southern West Bank. What one says, and how one says it, whether with a semblance of truthfulness or without it, whether with the minimal humility that being human demands, or without it—all this is the stuff of speech in the desert. If your mind is sticky with old myths, like most human minds, and if the myth speaks through your voice, sooner or later you will be laughed off those hills. I have heard many lies spoken by soldiers, policemen, bureaucrats, settlers, and, of course, politicians in situations where Palestinians can, by virtue of their predicament, only speak their truth. In other, less fraught scenarios, they, Palestinians, can, of course, tell lies—but not at a moment of incipient or recurrent expulsion and exile, which has the inevitable effect of revealing truth, though the soldiers and policemen and their allies may not want, or be able, to hear or see it.

Stark natural beauty, truthfulness, intimacy, love: these elements are bound together in a single sorrowful amalgam. It is important to remember them, in case the Israeli government has its way and the Palestinians of South Hebron are one day finally and irrevocably driven away. It is important to know that once there was a way of life, natural to this landscape, where together these vectors met and enhanced one another. Things are a little different in the towns and cities. But the core compound is not yet exhausted. I would want to add to it a further set of notions, such as courage, solitude, silence. I have learned to recognize these forces when I meet them in the field.

Courage is not, I think, something a person can know in himself or herself; it is something one notices in others. But solitude and silence, and their implications for living, are accessible to our self-awareness. I sometimes think I am happiest when I am walking, either alone or almost alone, under the sun and wind in South Hebron. I listen for the silence, which is never total, but which nonetheless can envelop the barking of dogs and the bleating of sheep and the birdcalls and also human sounds like children crying or wives chiding their husbands or even—much graver in consequence—a mother screaming at the officer who has just arrested her young son.

A dimension of solitude inheres in the heartscapes of South Hebron. Many of the shepherds and farmers live in small *khirbehs*, a tent or two planted somewhere on a hill, maybe with a goat pen attached, preferably somewhere close to a still usable well. Such places are isolated and extraordinarily vulnerable. Nights, in particular, are scary. Men with guns may turn up. Even if they don't, a dense solitude defines this way of life. It is a solitude that informs the sociality of a pastoralist's existence on the cusp of the desert. Brothers, cousins, children, aging parents—all are somewhere nearby, one is not usually quite alone; but if you stay for some hours with these shepherds, and if you're lucky enough to pick a moment when the settlers or soldiers don't appear, you can't help but feel, in yourself, the brooding power of rock and sky. Still, the shepherd's life is utterly unromantic; his head is full of matters such as counting the goats and calculating their feed and where water will come from and how to fix the tent or shack he lives in and how to ensure there will be food tonight and who his cousin will find to marry, and also modern issues like how to buy a good phone and maybe study at some college—and, of course, on top of all of this, how to survive the settlers' attacks and the demolition orders routinely handed down by the Civil Administration. And there are common medical concerns, not so simple to handle out on the hills.

As many have noted—Thoreau again—solitude is conducive

to a mode of truthfulness. It's also possible that enough solitude may be conducive to courage. I am often astonished to
see how young shepherds respond to the soldiers. Sometimes
these boys are clearly frightened; sometimes, especially after
violent incidents have taken place, or threats uttered against
them, they cling to us, asking us repeatedly to stay close to
them, for their protection. One can understand that. The soldiers sometimes threaten to shoot them if they come back into
such and such a wadi, or use some now forbidden well. But
very often, more often I think, the boys are clearheaded and
defiant. They can be forced to obey the arbitrary commands of
the officers, and they know the potentially high cost of arrest.
But the mere fact that these people are still in place, despite the
vast forces that have been brought to bear upon them, speaks
to a toughness that comprises within it a stubborn courage. In
a way, it's their greatest asset.

There is something about being there that opens up your
heart. The clenched, embattled quality that is our standard
point of departure slowly dissipates, over a morning or a day or
a night. It's not something that happens in the thinking mind.
It's not something you can program or strive for. All of us, however, know it, though we may never speak about it to one another. Usually, we are caught up in the exigencies of the given
moment—the Border Police officer who draws an arbitrary
line in the sand and says, "Whoever steps over this border will
be arrested;" the bureaucrat from the Civil Administration who
stops the plowing and says, "Not today" or "not here" or "not
there" or "not anywhere;" the settler who rushes into the herd
of goats and sends them fleeing toward the desert; the roadblock that has to be taken down, at whatever cost; and so on.
In such circumstances, one's mind works full time. And still: a
dimension of feeling arises somewhere in the lower reaches of

the body and, from time to time, reaches upward toward the stubborn sense of who one is. There is a lot of thinking to be done, and there are often risks to calculate, and hard choices. You also see manifest suffering and unmistakable wickedness and much foolishness. Through it all, there is the welcome yet surprising opening of the heart. The friendships we have forged depend upon it and make sense of it. But of friendship I may speak another time.

Of one thing I am certain, and not in some mental mode of judgment but as an Aurelian form of knowledge. The price exacted by the Occupation from Israeli Jews is beyond reckoning. My life in Israel coincides exactly with the life of the Occupation; I have seen it mutate from harsh military rule at its inception to the inferno of violent theft and state terror that is in place today. It embodies wickedness of such intensity that it calls into question the legitimacy and viability of the state itself. Worse even than that, it has corroded the souls of thousands, possibly millions. Let me proclaim, again, the principle that seemed a little tentative at the start of this essay, and that now seems incontrovertible. One cannot violate the inner being of an entire people without violating and impoverishing one's own inner life. The universe has its laws. Israelis need to be liberated from the Occupation no less than the Palestinians need to become free.

7

FINAL REFLECTION

On Resistance

For now, perhaps forever, there is work to be done—outside in the world, also inside ourselves. For me, at least, the latter mode is insistent. I live with doubt, as I hunger for truth. All of us in Israel-Palestine have been living for decades with much wickedness and many lies.

You may have noted the tools we forged, mostly improvising from scratch, in these long years of what looks like hopeless struggle. I'd like to think they could be useful to others who face similar states of severe oppression and who cannot turn away from at least trying to do the decent thing, insofar as they can determine what that is. Sometimes it's very plain. Often, recalcitrant ambiguity envelops the choice. Usually, the end, if there is an end, seems to recede as one approaches it. As everyone knows and many have said, every generation has to fight its own fights for freedom, surely the most powerful of all human needs and by far the most elusive.

I began with the goodness of despair—the kind of despair that can serve as a catalyst to action, not the kind that allows you to slip into the soporific passivity that may well be our natural default. I think despair was my own, personal starting point. It deepened and worsened over the years, until I was forced from within to do something useful with it. I discovered it could serve as my instrument, my friend and companion. I also discovered its unexpected beauty, once I was able to use it—the strange beauty of fighting a hopeless battle. And again: the more hopeless it is, the more hope one generates in oneself by recycling despair, by embracing the inner and outer torment as a gift, for that is what it truly is. Among the many good things that life offers, there is the goodness of struggling uphill against impossible odds. Concrete results in the field do matter, but they are not the final criterion. I'll come back to this point one last time.

I had a friend who died young. His name was Jonathan Frankel. He was an adventurer and a fine historian. Perhaps the last words he said to his wife were: "Sail into the wind." I often think of those words. They ring true. One who has never known the sheer joy of sailing into the wind may not understand.

Those words describe what we do in South Hebron and the Jordan Valley. No matter how many successes we have on the microlevel—the fields we have restored to their owners, the villages we have saved, the homes we have rebuilt, the innocents we have kept from arrest and torture—we are unable to change the political situation itself. Some day the Occupation will end, but it will not be because of our small victories. And yet, in my own sense of what all this means, it is the micro-moments that matter most. I identify strongly with the words of Marek Edelman, the last commander in the Warsaw Ghetto uprising; after the war he became a well-known cardiologist-surgeon in Poland. This is how he described his work: "God is trying to blow out the candle, and I'm quickly trying to shield the flame, taking advantage of his brief inattention. To keep the flame flickering, even if only for a little while longer than He would wish." The statement is of a piece with his earlier role in the murdered ghetto; the same logic rules them. We, too, are trying our best to keep the flame flickering.

But since I have now mentioned a truly heroic figure, I hasten to say once more that our own work is entirely antiheroic. It has nothing in common with the heroic virtues, however one defines them. Indeed, the chimera of romantic heroism is certain to ruin any genuine effort on the ground. What is needed, above all, is a mode of dogged, dull persistence. If I am lucky, I can sometimes remember—while being blocked by the soldiers, or humiliated, or physically poked and pushed off some piece of stolen land, or worse than any of the above—that this, too, counts as sailing into the wind. More often, that awareness kicks in much later.

What that means in practice is that along the way there are endless failures; also, at times, serious mistakes. However, it is definitely possible to cultivate stubbornness. They knock you down; you rise again. It happens many times. All of us have learned to contain the hurt, the outrage, and—possibly worse—the boredom of routine defeat. We also know that if we persist, week after week, there is a good chance that we will ultimately succeed in regaining some lost hill now overgrown with brambles or fenced off by settlers. "Ultimately" is not, however, the best word, because such successes are frequently tenuous and have to be fought for again and again in the face of continuous attempts by the settlers and soldiers to reverse them.

Dogged persistence is one important rule of thumb.

At times I wake in the middle of the night, when the world looks most dark. At such moments, I may think to myself: It's all mad, just as the officer rightly said to me when we were trying to bring the goats to the well.[21] So why tinker with little bits and pieces? Sooner or later the Palestinian shepherds will be swept away, perhaps not, after all, by the Civil Administration and the Israeli police and the settlers but by time and history. Why, then, fight to keep them on their lands for another generation or two? Of course, I know that I am there for Nasser and Eid and Sa'id and many others and that I will do whatever I can do—anything—to help them. Indeed, quite apart from helping them, I know I must be there with them, and that *being with* could be the best name for what we do in South Hebron. But I also, sometimes, remember Marek Edelman.

Another tenuous flame to cultivate is ironic joy. In this business, irony is no less useful than despair. It comes along with a singular kind of happiness. I think an irony-infused joy must be akin to what Socrates says to Phaedrus about "the words that are inscribed in the soul of the student, that can fight for themselves and that know before whom one must be silent."[22] Words, that is, that become who we are, not merely the (reduced and recorded) shadow or reflection of who we are. Words that carry the surpassing vision that Socrates has defined as the true mark of love, or of wisdom. Is there any way that, for us, such words could be anything but ironic? We act from within the irony, the exact opposite of an earnest innocence. When doubt comes, irony will carry you through.

Sometimes people ask me if I am not afraid. I don't know how to answer. Usually, we struggle more with frustration and weariness and, sometimes, boredom—than with fear. At moments, however, all of us have experienced sudden surges of fear, or even of terror. It can happen within seconds. Physical violence is an ever latent threat to the activists (and to all Palestinians in the occupied territories). So yes, I am sometimes afraid. Then it is a matter of what one does with fear. In this, fear is a lot like despair, in the sense that a potentially

paralyzing emotion can be used to good effect if one is prepared to act from within in, not simply succumbing or receding
into oneself. The body thinks first, then the heart. Fortunately,
in real emergencies fear gets washed away in doing what has to
be done and caring for others.

Some of you who are reading these words will already be
part of some similar struggle; others may be drawn in over
time. You don't need advice from me. The tools are already in
your hands; urgency and necessity will whet them. For what
it's worth, I do my best not to judge our enemies too harshly,
and not to hate them, even if I hate what they are doing. The
world is already too deeply split into antinomies of black and
white; this splitting may even be the root cause of most of our
misery. As I have said, the worst danger facing those who work
these furrows is to fall into self-righteousness and sentimental
moralism.

Moralistic judgment is the dark underside of moral action.
I try to put the first aside in the interests of furthering the second. It's not easy. I have to remind myself often that a genuine
moral act is its own goal and requires no further rationale,
though I am also sure, now, after years of fighting the Occupation, that an act of goodness—any such act—eventually has
further benevolent consequences. I have many times seen a
tiny gesture of kindness expand until it reaches out to the lives
of many. There are lands that have been saved from the settlers
because shepherds somewhere in the West Bank have heard
from friends about Ta'ayush and what we do. But in general, we
may not live to see such happy consequences. This knowledge,
though also not lacking in irony, sometimes sustains me.

I never forget that I have a choice, and I hold on fiercely
to that slight edge of freedom, the margin that each of us has,
though many prefer not to know it. That is where my con-

science lives. I, too, often fail. I think, for example, of Uday, a young shepherd from al-Hammeh in the Jordan Valley. Not long ago he was out on the hills with the sheep and goats, and settlers came and hit him hard on the forehead with a heavy rod. Since then, he has been in bad shape. The doctors say he has permanently lost 40 to 60 percent of his vision, among other severe problems. We should have been with him that day, though we can't be everywhere, and some of us are only in the field from time to time, when we can get away. If we had only been there. . . . But we can be with him now, and maybe we can still stop the next attack, or meet the violence together with its intended victims, whenever it comes. Maybe we can do something useful, in our own small way, for truth — by bearing witness, by not turning away. Truth, surprisingly, requires such assistance. The alternative is not appealing. It's not so hard a choice.

8

CODA

Iftar *at Sarura*

June 26, 2017

I know what it's like to clean out a cave. I've done it myself, one among many volunteers. Many of the people of the South Hebron hills used to live in caves, but over the years, beginning in the late 1990s, the army drove them out and then stopped up the caves with rock and sand and debris. Each such cave was a home—often a spacious and comfortable home, cool in the burning summer, warm in the frozen winter. Often the shepherds shared the cave with their goats and sheep, who inhabited a space of their own near the entrance.

It can take days of hard work to clear a cave of the rubble and rock the army bulldozers have dumped there. One carries bucket after bucket of sand and stones up to the surface, and even when most of the debris has been removed there remains the work of sweeping and fixing and cleaning and laying down a new floor and paving the entrance and building the stone parapet on either side of the entrance. You need a team of strong workers undaunted by the endless dirt and the fierce heat outside. In the South Hebron hills, there is also the constant danger that settlers or soldiers will drop by to put an end to the whole effort; that the bulldozers will appear and block up the cave once more, that the soldiers will point their guns at you and threaten you with all the worn-out words of hate and terror, and that when they go away you will have to start all over again.

But at Sarura, working steadily over four to five weeks, the Palestinian families and a remarkable coalition of peace groups and volunteers succeeded in renovating two beautiful caves. They worked through Ramadan—the Palestinians fasting by day. The army carried out three very violent raids, destroying whatever they could, confiscating tents, mattresses, food, water, impounding a car, physically assaulting the activists, threatening arrests: the usual protocol. So there was havoc and rage and fear, and despite it all the caves are habitable again, and Ramadan is over, and we are here to celebrate the post-fast meal, the *iftar*. It is not every day that we have such victories.

Sarura sits on a rocky ridge overlooking the desert to the east and the threatening Israeli settlement of Chavat Maon, all too close. Its lands are owned by the Haraini, al-'Amar, Hamamdi, and Raba'i families; they have Ottoman-period land deeds to prove it. Over time the violence of the settlers and harassment by the army became unbearable; still, the families continued to work the land and to graze their sheep there, maintaining a continuous presence. Sometimes they would sleep in the caves, those the army had not entirely destroyed.

Then, on May 19th, 2017, they began cleaning out the caves together with volunteers from the Popular Resistance Committee of the South Hebron Hills, the Holy Land Trust from Bethlehem, All That's Left: Anti-Occupation Collective, the Center for Jewish Non-Violence (these last two founded by and largely comprised of North American activists), and the Combatants for Peace, among others, with active support from Ta'ayush and Haqel. Activists from Belgium and Toronto and Australia and Tel Aviv converged on Sarura; on weekends, there were hundreds here. During these last weeks, including all of Ramadan, they created the Sumud Freedom Camp on this bleak hilltop, a tiny dot in the vastness of heat and stone. *Sumud:* perseverance, holding fast. They worked together, they held workshops on the modes and means of nonviolent resistance, they shared the evening *iftar* meals. Volunteers slept here every night and stood guard during the day. It worked. Hard days lie ahead.

Battle-hardened Israeli peace activists have learned something new from their North American and other international counterparts. For example, there's a nonchalant toughness that can take your breath away. They know what they're doing, and why, and they're not afraid. You know what? I think there is, after all, a limit to how long you can terrorize millions of innocent human beings, kill them with impunity, rob them of their rights, their dignity, and their possessions, drive them from their homes into the desert. Even if the government eventually decides to root out this irksome reminder of its own continuous malice, the Sarura model will survive.

Fadil Abu Fuad has a deep scar on his nose. One of the soldiers hit him hard with his rifle. As he tells me the story of Sarura, I dream that someday I will see the soldier who struck him, and the cursed officer who gave the order, in the dock of the International Court of Justice in the Hague. That day may yet come.

"I was born on April 1st, 1962—in Sarura, right over there. [He points to a distant pile of rocks on the hill.] My father, too, was born here, in that cave [pointing north over the ridge], sometime in the nineteenth century. My father's father was born here, and so on back into the depths of time. I grew up here, I married here, and my first three sons were born here. I myself own fifty dunams of land in the village, and 350 dunams farther east, on the way into the desert, the direct bequest of my father. We are shepherds and farmers; I grew up among the sheep and goats.

The settlers came and tormented us every day; it got worse and worse, and the soldiers joined them in making our lives miserable. By 1997 only a few of us were left in the caves. I lived for some time in Twaneh, but the sheep were here; we never abandoned this place. We always came to graze the herds, we plowed and sowed seeds. It was very difficult. The settlers—from Chavat Maon, just over that hill—blocked up our wells. We had no water. It was a continuous struggle to hang on. We had help from the Italian Dove team and others, and then Ta'ayush arrived and stood by us and protected us. They brought us water, since the wells were gone. They worked beside us.

The courts offered no justice and no help. Then, a few years ago, settlers killed thirty-five of my sheep and burned our tents and all the fodder we'd saved for the herd. We knew we had to be here, whatever happened, otherwise the village would be lost forever. On May 19th we began clearing the caves, together with these activists and volunteers. They are strong and determined. We worked together. I dug with my own hands a deep well that can hold 150 cubic meters.

The soldiers came and destroyed whatever they could, and one of them struck me on my face, hard, with his gun, and they confiscated my car. Now they want me to pay fifteen thousand shekels to get it back. Where can I find that kind of money? Ramadan has come and gone, and with God's help we will stay. This is our land. We will live here until we die. No settler and no soldier will drive us out. Only God's will could uproot us. We welcome all of you, without titles and even without names. All of us are one today."

You should hear those words together with what Isaac Kates Rose said during the *iftar* speeches. He was speaking about the second time the army visited the Sarura camp, on May 22nd, with the obvious aim of breaking it up. "We were five internationals, five Israelis, five Palestinians. There were about thirty soldiers. To put it succinctly: we won. Fadil Abu Fuad was my teacher that day. I grew up in Toronto, and as a child my body had learned to idolize Jewish bodies holding big guns. But when the soldiers came in the middle of the day, marching down the hill, scaring the kids who were playing, in that moment I had a new language teacher and I learned a new language. I looked at Fadil, who showed me that he had in his own body all he needed to resist. Come, he said to me, we will hold on to this tent and not let go of it, and we will hold on to one another and not let go. And here we are: still holding fast. We have built relationships on trust and respect. I believe these relationships have world-historical meaning. Such relationships, rooted in nonviolent resistance, will break the Occupation. We stand together in the South Hebron hills to build a future of freedom."

It is late afternoon: hot, fiery, dry, dusty, with sudden gusts of sand-clogged wind that tears at your eyes and ears. Maybe we are only shouting into the wind. But everyone knows that something unprecedented has happened. Two caves are clean, freshly swept, spacious, livable, cool. And there is the road— they have begun to renovate the pit-filled road. So there is rebuilding this village, in the face of the virulent authorities and the violent settlers, and at the same time the building of a community, reconnected to Mufagara on the next ridge and Twaneh and Susya and Tawamin, and tightly bound to all the organizations that joined together to make this moment happen. It's part of a wider process slowly unfolding with our help, year after year, of coming home and being at home—in Bi'r al-'Id and Susya and Tawamin and Teku'a, a reversal of all that the Occupation stands for and all that it wants.

That's why when Riyad Halees from the Combatants for Peace begins to speak, we hear in his voice the sober delirium of truth: "We declare today that Sarura is free, a place of liberation, where those who live here can assume their responsibilities, for peace comes only with the duty to protect it in the face of all those who wish us harm." The wind whips at his lips. I think of other, more famous declarations of independence and the lurking dangers that have overtaken them. Hafez al-Haraini, my old friend, completes the thought. "Together we are making a change. We have shown the effectiveness of joint nonviolent struggle. You who have joined us—your presence here is more powerful than all the guns of the Occupation. We thank you. We will never give up, *lam nistaslim.*"

And then we danced. It's not so often you get to see Palestinians truly happy, except at weddings. Fadil dances like no one else. For long minutes I dance with him, up and down, over the rocks and sand. It wasn't just me. You could touch or taste in the air the uncanny joy given, rarely, to human beings when they emerge intact from the enveloping miasma of wickedness and sorrow. *Sa'ada*, happiness: the word on everyone's lips this afternoon. There is no happiness like home.

A little hesitant, I ask Sophie Schor, who's been here from the start, if she feels she's part of a historic moment. She's in no rush to say yes. She knows we're looking at one tiny crack in the wall. She knows about time. These things take time. They rise and fall. Then she says: "There's a community here beyond anything I've ever experienced." She's got the unpretentious toughness and insouciance of this new generation of activists. They don't say it, but I know: there will be other Saruras.

Sometimes, not so rarely, when the light turns gold just before dark, and you can hear the desert breathing like a living thing, and you're not alone any more, and a kind of bodily knowing sets in, unlike any other, and fear evaporates, and you stop counting up this thing and that, you get the unsolicited salty taste of freedom on your tongue.

NOTES

1   *Lā yuslīka ka'l-ya'si.* Translation courtesy of Iyas Nasser.

2   See above, pp. 40–41.

3   See the report above, pp. 36–44.

4   Neville Symington, *The Blind Man Sees: Freud's Awakening and Other Essays* (London: Karnac, 2004), 205.

5   See p. 34.

6   Thus Sureśvara, *The Realization of the Absolute: The "Naiṣkarmya Siddhi" of Śrī Sureśvara*, trans. A. J. Alston (London: Shanti Sadan, 1971).

7   The Druze, an Islamic sect, live mostly in villages in the Galilee; their men serve in the Israeli army.

8   Breaking the Silence, *Our Harsh Logic: Israeli Soldiers' Testimonies from the Occupied Territories, 2000–2010* (New York: Metropolitan, 2012).

9   My thanks to Charles Hallisey for discussion of this point.

10 Hannah Arendt, *The Life of the Mind* (New York: Harcourt, 1978), 217; and see Sharon Sliwinski, *Dreaming in Dark Times: Six Exercises in Political Thought* (Minneapolis: University of Minnesota Press, 2017), 41–43.

11 Hannah Arendt, *Between Past and Future: Eight Exercises in Political Thought* (New York: Penguin, 1968), 156.

12 On the false antinomy: "Our freedom, it is said, is either total or nonexistent. This dilemma belongs to objective thought and its stable-companion, analytical reflection. . . . But we have learnt precisely to recognize the order of phenomena. We are involved in the world and with others in an inextricable tangle. . . . Nothing determines me from outside, not because nothing acts upon me, but, on the contrary, because I am from the start outside myself and open to the world."

Maurice Merleau-Ponty, *Phenomenology of Perception*, trans. Colin Smith (London: Routledge and Kegan Paul, 2000), 454–66.

13   Immanuel Kant, *Critique of Practical Reason*, trans. Thomas Kingsmill Abbott (London: Longmans, Green & Co., 1889), 99–100.

14   Symington, *The Blind Man Sees*, 184.

15   Fyodor Dostoyevsky, *The Brothers Karamazov*, trans. Andrew M. MacAndrew (New York: Bantam, 1970), 339.

16   See above, pp. 4–6.

17   Kant knew this well: "Now all *belief* is a conviction of truth which is subjectively adequate but *consciously* regarded as objectively inadequate; it is therefore treated as the opposite of *knowledge*." "What Is Orientation in Thinking?," in Kant, *Critique of Practical Reason*, 244.

18   In Gregory Hays's beautiful translation of Marcus Aurelius' *Meditations* (New York: Modern Library, 2003), 43.

19   Vladimir Jankélévitch, *The Bad Conscience*, trans. Andrew Kelley (Chicago: University of Chicago Press, 2015), 35.

20   Spinoza's *Ethics* 3.11 note (trans. R. H. M. Elwes, http://www .gutenberg.org/files/3800/3800-h/3800-h.htm). My thanks to Yohanan Grinshpon for discussing this passage with me.

21   See pp. 150–51.

22   Plato, *Phaedrus* 276a (trans. B. Jowett, http://www.gutenberg.org /cache/epub/1636/pg1636.txt).

BIBLIOGRAPHY

Arendt, Hannah. *The Life of the Mind.* New York: Harcourt, 1978.

————. *Between Past and Future: Eight Exercises in Political Thought.* New York: Penguin, 1968.

Breaking the Silence. *Our Harsh Logic: Israeli Soldiers' Testimonies from the Occupied Territories, 2000–2010.* New York: Metropolitan, 2012.

Bronner, Yigal. "Kafka in Area C." *Mondoweiss.* October 3, 2016.

Camus, Albert. *The Plague.* Translated by Stuart Gilbert. New York: Modern Library, 1947.

Cendrars, Blaise. *Oeuvres complètes.* Paris: Denoël, 1960–64.

Dostoyevsky, Fyodor. *The Brothers Karamazov.* Translated by Andrew M. MacAndrew. New York: Bantam, 1970.

Fondane, Benjamin. *Existential Monday: Philosophical Essays.* New York: New York Review of Books, 2016.

Jankélévitch, Vladimir. *The Bad Conscience.* Translated and with an introduction by Andrew Kelley. Chicago: University of Chicago Press, 2015.

Kant, Immanuel. *Critique of Practical Reason.* Translated by Thomas Kingsmill Abbott. London: Longmans, Green & Co., 1889.

Marcus Aurelius. *Meditations.* Edited and translated by C. R.

Haines. Loeb Classical Library 58. London: William Heine-
mann and G. P. Putnam's Sons, 1916.

———. Translated by Gregory Hays. New York: Modern Library,
2003.

Merleau-Ponty, Maurice. *Phenomenology of Perception.* Translated by Colin Smith. London: Routledge and Kegan Paul,
2000.

Plato. *Phaedrus.* Translated by B. Jowett. http://www.gutenberg
.org/cache/epub/1636/pg1636.txt.

Shulman, David. *Dark Hope: Working for Peace in Israel and Palestine.* Chicago: University of Chicago Press, 2007.

Sliwinski, Sharon. *Dreaming in Dark Times: Six Exercises in
Political Thought.* Minneapolis: University of Minnesota Press,
2017.

Spinoza, Benedict. *Ethics.* Translated by R. H. M. Elwes. http://
www.gutenberg.org/files/3800/3800-h/3800-h.htm.

Sureśvara. *The Realization of the Absolute: The "Naiṣkarmya
Siddhi" of Śrī Sureśvara.* Translated by A. J. Alston. London:
Shanti Sadan, 1971.

Symington, Neville. *The Blind Man Sees: Freud's Awakening and
Other Essays.* London: Karnac, 2004.

Wittgenstein, Ludwig. *Tractatus Logico-Philosophicus.* Translated
by David Pears and Brian McGuinness. London: Routledge,
1961.